THE BLESSING OF TEARS

The Blessing of Tears

Julie Sheldon

CANTERBURY
PRESS
Norwich

© Julie Sheldon 2004

First published in 1996 by Hodder and Stoughton Ltd

This edition published in 2004 by the Canterbury Press Norwich
(a publishing imprint of Hymns Ancient & Modern Limited,
a registered charity)
St Mary's Works, St Mary's Plain,
Norwich, Norfolk, NR3 3BH

www.scm-canterburypress.co.uk

British Library Cataloguing in Publication data

A catalogue record for this book is available
from the British Library

ISBN 1-85311-572-X

Printed and bound by
Bookmarque, Croydon

This book is dedicated to our daughters Mimi and Georgie

I always rather wanted to call this book 'Rivers of Mascara'! It seemed to sum up everything about tears, but as a friend pointed out it excluded the men. Having been trained as a professional ballet dancer this thought hadn't occurred to me as many of the men I knew wore mascara daily, but it was a good point and I didn't want *anyone* to feel they couldn't read this book just because the title had a 'girly' feel to it.

Tears are messy and generally one of those things we just 'don't do' in front of other people. We often feel the need to apologise when we cry and I think that is because we appear so vulnerable. To be vulnerable actually means to be *helpless, unprotected, wide open and defenceless* – all words that don't sit very comfortably with our culture of being stoical and 'in control'. Yet it's often at these times of extreme vulnerability, when a situation has appeared hopeless and you've tried everything that's humanly possible and there is nowhere else to turn, that you come to the end of 'self' and cry out to God for his help.

I had almost finished writing this book when we learnt that our younger daughter was seriously ill. Suddenly everything I had been researching about tears, all the different types and reasons for crying, came to life. I began to experience and live each chapter in a way that became a real source of comfort and understanding. By reading other people's experiences, and seeing their vulnerability, I found myself being helped and strengthened in a way I couldn't have imagined.

I offer my sincere thanks to all those who have contributed to this book.

Contents

Contents

Foreword by Nicky Gumbel

In 1991 I read an article in the *Evening Standard* about Julie Sheldon, a former ballet dancer. By the age of sixteen, Julie was dancing with the Royal Ballet in a Gala performance with Margot Fonteyn and Rudolf Nureyev in front of the Queen Mother. In 1986, she contracted Dystonia, a neurological disease which within three years left her crippled and fighting for her life.

As she lay in her hospital bed, a friend brought Cannon Jim Glennon to pray for her. Later that same day she sat up in bed, unaided, for the first time in many months. Eight weeks later she threw away her crutches for good and had no more use for her wheelchair. Professor David Marsden, a leading expert on Dystonia, described Julie's healing as a 'miraculous recovery'.

I often recommend Julie's book, *Dancer Off Her Feet*, before the talk on healing in the Alpha course at our church. It was a great joy to meet her when she came to speak at Holy Trinity Brompton. Her talk, as well as her first book, had a great impact on many people's lives and Julie has since become a good friend.

N. G.

1

A Crying Shame

Laugh and the world laughs with you;
Weep, and you weep alone
                    Ella Wheeler Wilcox (1855–1919)

Unfinished tears
are a partly used hanky
which, if stuffed away, rots.

Presenting
dry eyes to the world
causes the fabric within to weaken.

                                        Gail

I never used to cry in public. Smiling was what I did.
'Smile, girls, smile! The public will have paid very
good money to come and watch you perform. They
don't want to know about your bleeding toes and your
aching backs. Come on, now, let's see those teeth

1

and bright, sparkling eyes! Smile!'

The encouraging, if not a little painful, words of my old ballet mistress still easily come to mind twenty years after having left ballet school. I had longed to be a ballerina from the age of three, and had learnt pretty quickly about the discipline required to be a professional and dedicated dancer.

Ballerinas particularly attract adulation, as there is a sense of the ethereal with the movements looking so graceful and easy, wrapped around storylines that usually project her as the heroine or tragic lover. But after the final curtain call there may be quite a different story to act out.

One doesn't have to train for fifteen years to be a dancer to understand about failure and disappointment, and trying to attain perfection. The sense of jumping a little higher or stretching that tiny fraction more can metaphorically apply in other walks of life and professions, as can wearing a performer's 'mask'.

The public want the illusion to be maintained. The effort and struggle behind successful performance must be concealed. I was trained as much in hiding my true feelings as in dancing.

Years later, I had just finished giving a talk, and was feeling immensely relieved at having completed it without stumbling, drying up or coughing. I looked up with a smile, only to see rows and rows of people crying. I was completely taken aback. Faces were streaked with mascara, little bundles of tissues were dabbing at the corners of red eyes, large white hand-

kerchiefs slipped behind spectacles while simultane-
ously trying to catch drips from the ends of noses!
What on earth was going on? Why was everyone
crying? Had I missed something?

My ballet training had prepared me to face an
audience, but here was a roomful of over two hundred
people, many of whom were weeping – a situation
that no ballet mistress had ever trained me for!

I had been talking about my life as a ballet student,
and later as a sufferer from the severely crippling
neurological disease, dystonia. I was giving testimony
to God's healing, producing physical and emotional
wholeness, and somehow, through my telling this
story, God was creating an atmosphere that led to
tears.

A young man came forward, out of the gathering.
'I've searched the bookshelves in the shop looking for
something, anything, about tears,' he began, before I
even learnt his name! 'I'm a newly ordained deacon
and I was wondering if you could help me?' he
continued.

You see, every time I set foot in church, start to
pray, try to sing, in fact any time I come into
God's presence, I have this overpowering feeling
of wanting to weep. I don't know what's the
matter with me. It's becoming rather difficult as
I have to lead services and spend most of the
time fighting and choking back the tears. What
do you think is happening? I've been brought up

to think that men don't cry and that it's rather a weak thing to do. I'm not depressed. In fact I'm quite the opposite. I think I'm beginning to understand what it means to be 'moved to tears'.

Rather wistfully he finished, 'I wonder if other people experience this too?' The words of this man, who eventually disclosed his name was George, sparked off a desire in me to find out the answer to his questions as I too had been experiencing this type of weeping. The more I talked with people about this, the more I realised that being 'moved to tears' was something many people experienced, but went to great lengths to hide!

So many questions about tears formed in my mind:

Why do we cry at all?

How do people regard tears, both their own and those of others?

What does the Bible have to say about tears?

Do many people share the young deacon's experience?

Is there such a thing as the 'gift' of tears?

Is weeping part of being a prayerful Christian today?

Was the very thing I had been trained not to do actually a source of God's healing?

I began by asking, 'Why do we cry?', but I soon discovered that the English language is ambiguous here. The word 'cry' means both 'utter a shrill loud sound' and 'weep'.

The First Cry

There is one cry that is universally welcomed. The first cry of the newborn baby is an extremely special moment and one where the mother forgets the months of pregnancy, the discomforts of labour and delivery, and for a time nothing else on earth matters. While the new parents are enraptured, their baby is making that first great effort as an independent individual. The first breaths of life are extremely hard work!

Not all babies cry at birth, and I remember one of our daughters making a sort of 'bird cheep' noise instead of the lusty howl we were expecting. That led to parental panic! Tom and I asked each other, and the hospital staff, 'Is she all right?' 'What's wrong?' 'Why isn't she crying?' We were comforted by being told that some babies just begin to breathe quietly.

That first cry of life possibly expresses a real distress or pain. Being born can happen very suddenly – all wet and naked – being thrust into a cold, brightly lit and noisy world. No wonder the baby can seem so upset! Also a lot of distress, the experts believe, is due to a feeling of suffocation which may be present at the time of birth. There is still amniotic fluid in the mouth and that probably makes the baby take its first breath. What a relief! But after that moment of urging the newborn baby to cry the parents quickly find themselves wishing it would stop!

I remember as a new parent spending much time wondering 'Why do babies cry?', especially while trying to comfort one of our two daughters in the middle of the night! But as a baby cannot fend for itself, discomfort or pain evokes a cry for help. Our trusty book on baby care reassures us that there are three types of crying that a parent quickly begins to recognise. The ordinary, or hungry, cry is easily resolved by a feed. The panic cry, which can follow if the hungry cry has been ignored, is harder to comfort and the baby can get into a real state if the hunger need is not met. The pain cry cannot be ignored by anyone, and makes everyone around extremely anxious. This cry is especially worrying if the baby holds its breath and starts going blue.

Babies cry to make their needs known, with and without tears. But what of adults? Why do people shed tears? I went to a doctor for some basic facts about tears, and crying.

What Are Tears?

From the physiological point of view, tears are a slightly oily liquid. Our eyes are constantly being washed with this fluid produced by our lachrymal glands. This process lubricates the eyeball, cleansing dust and bacteria from it, and giving nutrition and oxygen to the cornea.

Tears can be divided into three main types. The first is the ongoing secretion to maintain the good health of our eyes. Second is the reflex production of tears, as when we have a piece of grit, or a small fly in our eye, or when we are peeling onions, and we 'weep' until the foreign body or irritation is removed. Third come tears in response to emotion. The ability to cry such tears is unique to the human race. No other animals exhibit emotional weeping.

In 1994 the findings of a study of the chemical composition of different types of tears was published (X. D. Martin and M. C. Brennan, 'Serotonin in human tears', *European Journal of Ophthalmology*, 4(3), 159–65). Serotonin is a chemical neurotransmitter. Recently developed antidepressant drugs such as Prozac aim to increase the amount of serotonin in the brain. The study compared the amount of serotonin in reflex tears and emotional tears, and relatively huge amounts of serotonin were found in emotional tears. This happens because when emotion is experienced, the hypothalamus in the brain releases several neurotransmitters, including serotonin. In emotional tears, the serotonin is the *messenger* to boost the volume of production of tears from the lachrymal sac.

Fay is a bereavement visitor and physiotherapist who has the privilege of sharing many tears of both pain and happiness. Fay's husband is manager of a hospice and they often witness the close similarities between sadness and joy. In the physiotherapy department Fay and her colleagues frequently treat patients for hyperventilation. This occurs when someone repeatedly tries to control or suppress their tears, which leads to a rapid shallow breathing that may become a chronic state of hyperventilating. This can be a very frightening condition if it gets out of control. It is caused by a change in the body chemistry and is a result of prolonged alteration of the blood gases through an altered breathing pattern. It gives many of the physical symptoms of anxiety.

Dr Gareth Tuckwell, past director of the Christian centre for medical and spiritual care known as Burrswood, has written that tears are a God-given way of expressing our deepest feelings, especially when our areas of pain and joy scream for expression in a way that brings release.

So far we have a physiological description of tears. Dr Paul Worthley, who gave me much of this information, added, 'Why do we need to cry? I don't know, but it *may be* that the production and release of serotonin which causes tears may be stimulated by tears.'

The tears I am most interested in, according to this medical analysis, are those associated with emotion. But I want to start with *not* crying, which was how I was trained.

No Tears, Please

The British cultural style, summarised in the 'stiff upper lip', is not new. In the time of Jesus, one of the most popular philosophies was 'stoicism'. Zeno taught that reason should be behind all human action. He believed that reason dictates that devotion to duty is the only virtue. Helping people, according to stoicism, is to be done not from love but from duty, because that way the pain of being hurt by such things as the ingratitude of others can be avoided.

Devotion to duty as a way of life has great appeal. Socially, it keeps the wheels of relationships moving efficiently, and in theory it produces indifference to wealth or poverty, pain or pleasure, success or misfortune. Emotionally, stoicism involves the repression of feelings, and actively discourages displays of emotion, such as tears. Stoicism is the thinking behind Rudyard Kipling's popular poem 'If—', and it continues to influence families, society and churches today.

As babies we cry, and in most cases our needs are understood and met. It's not until we grow up a bit that we start to cry for reasons other than just hunger or pain. When a favourite toy has been taken away by a brother, or sister, the howling can be intense! But it is when a child begins to talk that the real trouble starts. 'Daddy, they won't let me play in the sandpit. Why can't I join in their game?' 'Sarah is my best friend and now Jo has taken her away.' 'They call me "Dumbo" in the playground because my ears stick out.' The tears that go with these sort of hurts can take much longer to dry.

From an early age small boys, particularly, are exhorted to be big and brave and not to be a 'wimp' or 'wet' when they trip up and graze their knees for the umpteenth time. If there is bullying at school, boys can gain much more 'street cred' by keeping their heads down and not complaining to anyone. The sneak becomes a creep in the eyes of his peers and he learns very fast about keeping his feelings to himself. All this is carried into adult life where it is acceptable to have a jolly good laugh, but the 'big boys' certainly don't cry!

Little girls have it slightly differently. 'There, there, darling, it's all right. Have a good cry and you'll feel much better. How about a nice tube of sweets to help dry the tears!' Perhaps the girls learn at a tender age how to get their own way with the odd tear or two and certainly toddlers love the gallons of extra sympathy their irresistible little pout can bring!

Even by the age of eight or nine children are learning to hide their tears, and it's not until adolescence that the weeping returns, but with a different intensity! The wails of 'Oh, I'm so unattractive. No one will ever love me! Why is my hair so greasy? And who invented spots anyway?' are heard in many households. The transition from being able to curl up on Dad or Mum's knee and have a cuddle to physically being unable to fit on a lap, makes this stage harder to bear!

But somewhere during these formative years the world has told us that tears are a sign of weakness; that when we are hurt physically and emotionally we must stem the flow from our tear ducts and be brave.

Tears are embarrassing and messy for everyone around, and bit by bit we learn to shut down this incredibly releasing, cleansing and healing emotion. The make-up on the performer's face is set hard and the mask is ready to act out the performance of life.

I wrote an article entitled 'The Blessing of Tears' in the magazine, *Healing and Wholeness* (No. 16, Oct./ Dec. 1994), and invited readers to write to me if they had been blessed through tears. This book is theirs as much as it is mine, as many people responded to my invitation, and I have drawn deeply on their experiences. So throughout this book I include contributions from many different people. Some are happy for their full name to be used; some are identified only by their Christian names; and some names are here replaced by pseudonyms.

The first contribution is from Janet Crisp, who gave me a real insight into what it was like to grow up during the Second World War. Janet was eight years old when the war broke out and was evacuated several times over the following six years. She was sent to different relatives in 'safe areas' and along with many other 'war children' had it drummed into her that she must be brave and not cry during the separations and terrifying air raids. Family and school teachers alike, lovingly but firmly, told her, 'Janet, if you are brave, and don't cry, you will help win the war!' By implication, to cry would help lose the war. One can only imagine what effect the pressure of imagining they had the power to lose the war by crying had on

Janet and countless of her young contemporaries.

Daphne Higginson, too, was a child who rarely cried, partly because it was not the 'done thing' either at home or at school, but mostly because it was recognised as a sign of weakness. In later life, she joined a branch of the Foreign Service and it was there that she was trained *never* to show emotion. Nearly everyone was trained in logical debate, which she was expected to use, and any tears shed were regarded as a sign of regression back to childhood, so Daphne kept a very firm check on any crying!

'I think it was children who began to break down the barriers in the end,' said Daphne. 'After ten years I took up teaching, and drying the children's tears taught me that it was natural to cry!' When rheumatoid arthritis forced Daphne to give up her job, the years of pain began to force her back into 'old controls', and long stays in hospital pushed her into 'being brave'. But one day something 'snapped'. She remembers,

> I cried and cried for hours, and a young nurse sent for the hospital chaplain, but he arrived *three days* later by which time it was all over! The chaplain stood at the end of my bed and told me I had never grieved for the death of my mother, which was true, but I'm sorry to say, by that time, I had written him off as someone not able to help.

The stoic ideals were firmly in place when Daphne

went to stay at Crowhurst (a house belonging to the Divine Healing Mission).

> But one day, after attending an early morning service, I rushed back to my room and wept and wept. Somebody must have heard as they came into the room and kissed me. I broke up completely. Gradually the tears, unshed for so many years, came out, finally washing away the stoicism and stiff upper lip. Now I find it easy to weep and can even cry for joy!

A poem written by Dorothy Hsu – a young widow writing in the first year after her loss – sums up the stoical attitude to life, but hints at an alternative to stoicism, where she refers to the New Testament exhortation to rejoice and weep with others (Rom. 12:15).

> Sometimes I hate my smile.
> Why must it always interfere?
> It builds up a wall
> Just at those times when
> I want the barrier down.
> When I smile,
> Everyone else smiles,
> And then their gates clang shut, too.
>
> Why can't I be honest?
> Just once.

The Blessing of Tears

Why can't I let the tears flow
And expose my heart?
Why must I always act the stoic
And bear it alone?

You've commanded us
To 'rejoice with them that do rejoice,
And weep with them that weep'.

Surely someone would weep with me.
Surely someone would,
If only I could.

That longing to be real and honest with oneself and
other people is something I'm sure we would love to
be able to express more freely, but sadly the worldly
view is quite different. I was listening one afternoon
to a chat show on the radio where the actress Joan
Collins was being interviewed. The discussion was
mainly about diet and health tips, but of course the
conversation soon came around to the inevitable: 'I
have to ask you, Joan, and I know all the listeners will
long to know, *how* do you keep yourself looking so
fantastic?'

Joan demurely thanked the interviewer for her
compliment and then proceeded to explain, 'What you
look like on the outside totally represents what you
are inside. If you look beautiful, well-kept and
groomed, that shows you are peaceful inside.'

I found myself laughing out loud because that

thinking seemed so totally opposite to the Christian
viewpoint. No amount of make-up, designer clothes
or thinness will ever bring the truth that we are loved
and accepted by God – just as we are. In our society
we can dress up, eat up, drink up and hide behind all
sorts of disguises, but true and lasting inner peace,
love and joy come only from a relationship with God
through Jesus Christ. Sometimes the tears that
accompany the dawning of this revelation bring rivers
of mascara down our neatly powdered, stoic faces!

2

A Gathering of Tears

Record my lament;
  list my tears on your scroll/put my tears in
   your wineskin
  are they not in your record?

Psalm 56:8

Jesus wept.

John 11:35

God . . . will wipe every tear from their eyes.
There will be no more death or mourning or
crying or pain.

Revelation 21:3–4

The Old Testament includes many accounts of people crying at times of distress or other great emotion. David's grief and tears at the death of his son Absalom (2 Sam. 18:33–19:1) is a very familiar example of weeping at the loss of a loved one. Intense emotion on being reunited after separation was often accompanied by tears; for example, brothers Jacob and Esau (Gen. 33:4), and Joseph's reunions with Benjamin and his other brothers (Gen. 45:14–15) and with his father, Jacob (Gen. 46:29). Similarly, emotional partings were accompanied by tears, as at David and Jonathan's leave-taking (1 Sam. 20:41) and Naomi and her daughters-in-law saying farewell (Ruth 1:9).

Personal sorrows caused people to weep. Esau wept when he had been cheated out of his blessing (Gen. 27:38), Hannah wept because she was childless (1 Sam. 1:7, 10), Job's friends wept at the sight of his disfiguring sores (Job 2:12). Whole nations could mourn the death of a leader with collective weeping. This happened, for example, when Jacob died (Gen. 50:3), when Aaron (Num. 20:29) and Moses (Deut. 34:8) died, and after the deaths of Saul and Jonathan (2 Sam. 1:11f., 24).

Jeremiah is sometimes referred to as the 'weeping prophet', but he was not alone in weeping as part of his prophetic ministry over the sufferings of the people. See Isaiah 22:4; 24:4; Jeremiah 9:1; 13:17; 14:17; and Lamentations 1:2, 16; 2:18; 3:48 for examples of this. Nehemiah cried over ruined Jerusalem (Neh. 1:4). God notices tears, especially those that accompany beseeching prayer (2 Chr. 34:27; Isa. 38:5). The writer of Ecclesiastes laments the tears called forth by oppression (Eccles. 4:1).

The shedding of tears was such an important part

of showing grief for the Jews that professional mourners were hired at funerals (Jer. 9:17–22; Amos 5:16). Rabbi Judah ruled that 'Even the poorest in Israel should hire not less that two flutes (players to play a dirge) and one wailing woman'. People were actually employed to come and cry at funerals of wealthy families to help them work through their grief. Jesus referred to this when He commented on children's games of funerals and dancing (Luke 7:32).

The life and teachings of Jesus Christ present quite a contrast to the stoicism that was popular in His day. God, as portrayed in the Old Testament, was greatly concerned for those who were weeping. Jesus expands this to show a God who actually suffers with and beyond the suffering of His people. As both divine and human, Jesus clearly experienced and showed emotions, according to the Gospels. But the existence, let alone the depth, of these emotions is not always acknowledged, especially within the church. Jesus is frequently portrayed as though He had a stiff, stoic upper lip. How often people sing, and teach very small children, the familiar Christmas carol, 'Away in a manger', which includes 'The little Lord Jesus…no crying He makes'. But if Jesus cried as an adult He certainly cried as a child! Even Jesus, with all the powers that God gave Him to deal with people on an individual basis, speaking words of power, healing miraculously and acting out of love and compassion, could only cry when He was faced with the social, religious and political suspicions, hatred and injustices of His day.

Jesus's weeping over Jerusalem in Luke 19:41 shows how utterly overwhelmed by despair Jesus was for the city of God, holy Jerusalem. He is no stoic, but one who says, in the words of James Fleming, '*Your* hurt and *my* heart'. He was never indifferent to people's suffering. He raised the dead son of a widow in Nain to life again, because He 'had compassion for her' (Luke 7:13, NRSV). The word for 'compassion' here could almost be translated 'a gut reaction'. It is a physical thing, coming from internal body organs. At the time of Jesus, differing emotions were believed to arise from different parts of the body.

Dr James Fleming, director of the Jerusalem Centre for Biblical Studies, made a tape entitled 'The Tear Cup', in which he drew attention to the first-century custom of collecting and conserving tears in a tear cup, also known as a tear vase. The cup was tear-shaped, round and wide at the bottom with a long narrow neck leading to a flaring, circular rim. The rim was placed under the eye to catch tears as they were shed. The tear cup was then corked and stored.

The use of a vessel for saving tears is mentioned in the Bible in Psalm 56:8. In the NRSV the verse reads:

> You have kept count of my tossings;
> put my tears in your bottle.
> Are they not in your record?

Biblical scholars have commented on the poetic pun on the word here translated 'tossings' (elsewhere rendered 'wanderings') and the word 'bottle' which is usually translated as 'wineskin'. The psalmist cries out his personal pain to God, asking that his tears be kept carefully – a moving image of the depth of God's compassion and concern for His people.

There are three accounts in the New Testament that Dr Fleming alleges may refer to the collection of tears in a tear cup. The first is when Simon the Pharisee invited Jesus to dinner (Luke 7:36–50). The Pharisees' motive for loving God was out of duty to the law of Moses and therefore they looked down on such social outcasts as known sinners and tax collectors. During the meal at Simon the Pharisee's house, a public sinner arrived, bringing with her an alabaster jar full of perfume, and as she stood by Jesus's feet she began to weep. Her tears fell, wetting His feet, and then she dried them with her hair, kissed His feet and poured her perfume on them.

Because this woman was known as a sinner, Simon's duty to the law would keep him from associating with her, but Jesus had real compassion for her.

> Do you see this woman? I came into your house. You did not give me any water for my feet, but she wet my feet with her tears and wiped them with her hair. You did not give me a kiss, but this woman, from the time I entered, has not stopped

kissing my feet. You did not put oil on my head, but she has poured perfume on my feet. Therefore, I tell you, her many sins have been forgiven – for she loved much. But he who has been forgiven little loves little.

In Jesus's day the way someone showed they would like to be a particular rabbi's disciple was to offer to wash that rabbi's feet. The teaching the woman had heard from Jesus had so helped her that she literally flooded, and poured out, her tears on to His feet, releasing her past grief. The Jews did not separate body from soul; they believed how people feel physically affects their emotions, and emotions affect physiology. For them it was not grief that caused tears, but tears that cause grief. That is why they thought about saving the tears that cause grief. By putting them in a little cup they could be corked, and saved until the time when another tear-provoking thought came – perhaps, of a departed loved one. Then the tear cup would be opened, more tears would be cried, and saved.

This may seem a strange custom today to people who are inclined to say, 'Be brave, don't cry'; or even 'She's doing very well', when the bereaved person does not cry in their presence. First-century Jews would say to one another, 'Go on, cry. Here's a tear cup. Save your tears. Fill it up and we will get you another one.' The beautiful picture of the woman washing Jesus's feet with her tears may mean she no longer felt it necessary to save her past grief in a tear cup, but instead she poured out all her grief on Jesus's feet. Then Jesus said to her, 'Your sins are forgiven. Your faith has saved you; go in peace.'

Another incident from the Gospels which Dr Fleming believes may refer to the collection of tears in a tear cup is the death and raising of Lazarus (John 11). Lazarus was a dear friend to Jesus. His sisters, Martha, and Mary – who wiped Jesus's feet with her hair at the beginning of John 11, but who may not be the woman of Luke 7 – were completely distraught when their brother died. By the time Jesus arrived from the Jordan valley up to the village of Bethany near Jerusalem, Lazarus had been lying on a shelf in the tomb for four whole days. Martha and Mary had probably been crying all that time and as they went out to meet Jesus, He saw their tears as they were walking towards Him, and was deeply moved.

John 11:35, 'Jesus wept', is the shortest verse in the Bible. Perhaps that is why it has often been overlooked. Jesus was deeply moved by Mary's tears and wept when she invited Him to see where the body of her dead brother, Lazarus, had been laid. His tears of compassion, and perhaps anger, at death and bereavement, show quite clearly that He was no stoic (John 11:33). Perhaps He saw that their tear cups were full. I wonder if Jesus saw them in the distance carrying their tear cups? Jesus loved Martha and Mary, and He loved Lazarus and when He saw the sisters' tears of grief He was moved with compassion.

In the Garden of Gethsemane, shortly before being betrayed by Judas, Jesus prayed, 'Father, if it is possible, may this cup be taken from me' (Matt. 26:39). That cup has been identified in several different ways. It could represent a full cup of wine, either as a symbol of fate or a symbol of judgment. Or it could represent a tear cup full of tears, a symbol of sorrow. If this is so, Jesus's meaning may have been, 'The amount of grief and sorrow you are asking me to carry is a cup larger than I can bear.'

This unusual, but I think rather beautiful, custom of saving ones tears in a tear cup is a visual symbol of the healing that weeping brings. Deep sobs of grief produce tears. The full tear cup is the eventual relief for that grief – fill it up and you will be healed.

The five-year-old daughter of a missionary in Pakistan would sit on her father's knees when she was tired at the end of the day. Sometimes she would cry. Her father would take his big, dry, workman hands and catch each tear, saying, 'These tears are good for my hands and very precious.' By rubbing her tears into his rough hands, the father took the little girl's sorrow, and encouraged her to let her tears fall. He caught *each* tear.

As we have seen already, God has compassion on all those who weep. The following prophecy, given to Pat Rosamund, appeared in the magazine, *Prophecy Today*, (2(1), Jan./Feb. 1986) expressing how God views the tears of Christian believers. God sees such tears as precious jewels, rather than something of which Christians should be ashamed.

There are tears of joy in the lives of many, and these tears are like precious jewels as they cascade in a glitter of joyous light. Like fresh dewdrops cradled in green leaves in the early dawn, so the tears of joy and fulfilment in the eyes of my children are a precious witness to my joy and delight in them and their great joy and delight in me.

The tears of many sorrows are precious to me too; these are the tears I will wipe away, and when all sorrow is gone the jewel-like tears of joy will take their place. My children, you are in the world to help me with the tears of sorrow and anguish. It is your task for me to take love and compassion and the balm of my presence, to overcome the sorrows and trouble all around you.

The tears of joy I will count and keep as a treasure to open to you at the time of fulfilment, when with joy and gladness and praise and singing you will meet round my throne with me, and with all my children I have called by my name.

The crystal drops of tears of joy are the only tears known in heaven; the tears of the penitent will be wiped away. The tears of sorrow and pain and grief will be gently dried; and when all the tears of desperation and anguish and frustration have gone, I will bring forth in all their beauty and glory the tears of joy. Only the tears of joy can make you beautiful because they are the only beautiful tears. They dance and sing and sparkle as they fall, and they catch the colours of the sunlight in a glorious abandonment of rainbow colours, such colours as you cannot even dream of. There will be an enchantment of colour and light and love and you will be filled with a divine joy and happiness in my unveiled presence.

Your tears of joy are precious jewels to me and I am keeping them safe for you as you go about doing my work in the place where I have called you to be. The many tears of life in this world surround you; all are transitory; only the tears of joy are from everlasting to everlasting.

If each tear that falls is viewed as a jewel that is being kept safe in heaven, what a different perspective it gives to those who feel they must suppress their weeping. Fay gave me a beautiful illustration of this picture of our tears being stored in heaven. Using magnification in a laboratory you can watch a droplet falling into liquid and forming a coronet. Each tear surrendered into God's cup of suffering forms a tiny sparkling crown as it falls. In turn these little coronets make up the jewels in the crown that form part of the mystery of suffering. But that picture becomes one of victory and triumph, sadness turned into joy as each tear is surrendered.

Jesus accepted God's cup of suffering before His death. Graham Kendrick's song, 'The Servant King', sums this up:

> There in the garden of tears
> My heavy load He chose to bear,
> His heart with sorrow was torn,
> Yet not my will, but yours, He said.

Jesus was willing to release His blood and tears to accompany a different kind of crown, the crown of thorns.

A few years ago Fay experienced the sorrow of losing her twin brother. Now she remembers, looking back over her own bereavement journey, the occasion that was a turning-point in her grief: 'real "releasing" weeping at a service at which prayers were said for healing'. It was as if the crown of thorns of suffering and loss that had been cutting into her head became a jewel-studded crown instead. 'I have seen tears as "jewels" which have a special healing quality of the body, mind and spirit,' she wrote.

We recently took our daughters to the Tower of London to see the crown jewels. Apparently the two most common questions which visitors from all over the world ask the jewel-house wardens at the Tower are: 'Are the crown jewels real?' and 'How much are they worth?' The way the crowns are displayed brings out the best of each jewel; they sparkle, twinkle and glitter. They made me gasp at their beauty, and as the pieces are so rare I quickly realised the crown jewels are beyond price. I couldn't, at first, account for the fact that this visit to the Tower made me think of the young deacon, George, but it was probably the thought of him being embarrassed by something that should be regarded as precious that caused my mind to wander from the display cabinets. Perhaps one day he will see all the tears he has shed being gathered up into a 'crown of jewels', and his weeping will be accepted as a treasure, something of beauty and immense value.

3

Those Who Mourn

Oh eyes, no eyes, but fountains fraught with
tears

Thomas Kyd (1558–94)

When Mary Magdalene arrived at the tomb on the
first Easter morning, just imagine the shock she must
have had to discover the stone to the tomb had been
rolled away, and the body of Jesus had gone. I can
picture her running back to the disciples in a blind
panic, and with despair and desolation saying to them,
'They have taken the Lord out of the tomb and we
don't know where they have put him!' (John 20:2).

Later on, after the disciples had seen for themselves that indeed Jesus's body had gone missing,
Mary remained at the tomb. The image of her
weeping, tears coursing down her cheeks, as she
looked once more into the empty tomb, is a picture of
grief and great sadness, and shows the depth of her

sorrow in that she hardly seemed terrified of the two angels dressed in white sitting where Jesus's body had been laid out. When those angels spoke to her and asked, 'Woman, why are you crying?' Mary replied simply, 'They have taken my Lord away and I don't know where they have put Him.' The sense of loss through Jesus's tortured death compounded by the absence of His body had numbed Mary until nothing else mattered, not even speaking angels! She just wanted to know where Jesus was.

Then another man appeared behind her and asked the same question, 'Woman, why are you crying?' Because Mary thought this was the gardener she replied this time, 'Sir, if you have carried Him away, tell me where you have put Him and I will get Him.' I can hear the desperation and the pleading in her voice as this poor woman longed to find Jesus's body.

The man, Jesus, gently said, 'Mary.'

Immediately, Mary recognised Him and cried out, 'Rabboni' (teacher), and I love to think of Mary's sad crumpled face suddenly lighting up, eyes wide, and tears instantly stopped! The moment her name was spoken it was as if her whole life had been brought back together; the grief and sadness and dreadful loss had all vanished. Her name, spoken by Jesus, cut through the sobs and the weeping, because although Mary didn't recognise Jesus physically, her heart leapt when He used her name and immediately she was filled with joy and the knowledge that this *was* Jesus. I wonder if Mary had been crying so much that her eyes were swollen and puffy and maybe she just couldn't see through the haze!

Have you ever cried so much that you couldn't see through the haze? Sometimes we're unable to recognise Jesus standing there, beside us, because our grief and sense of loss is so overwhelming.

I experienced this sense of my name being used to cut through the haze when I was suffering with dystonia. One of the ways to relieve the pain was to be given nerve blocks into my legs, and sometimes into the spine as well. Because the injection, or block, was put into the nerve itself it meant a light general anaesthetic was needed each time. Therefore, on twenty occasions I went through a ritual each morning of being starved, because of the anaesthetic, and wheeled up to theatre to have the nerve blocks. Sometimes this was extremely successful, and all the pain was removed and the tremor in my legs subsided. On other days the nerve block did not seem to take effect, and the jolts and pain remained. Often I had the nagging thought, 'Was this all worth it to have a few pain-free hours?'

Something that stays with me from those frightening days, occasionally returning in the middle of the night, is the way the nurses would call my name in the recovery room as the anaesthetic was wearing off. 'Julie, Julie? Hello, Julie.' However deep the chemical slumber I was always aware, even before the pain did or did not return, of my name being spoken. It was if my name cut through the haze, through the tears and pain, and I responded to it.

The promise of God is this: 'I have called you by name' (Isaiah 43:1). He knows us before we are even born (Psalm 139:13) so whatever the suffering, like Mary's utter despair and loss, or our own pain and fear, Jesus *is* there calling each one of us by *our* name. It's just that sometimes we fail to recognise Him through the haze.

There is one occasion when modern Western culture does expect and accept tears, and that is in the agony of bereavement. This experience touches everyone sooner or later. But death is often a taboo subject, and sometimes Christians have a great deal more difficulty dealing with it than they care to admit. God's ultimate promise is of a place beyond death where 'He will wipe every tear from their eyes. There will be no more death or mourning or crying or pain' (Rev. 21:4).

This verse from Revelation helped Eileen Portsmouth to bring understanding to the terrible tragedy that struck her family when her four-year-old daughter, Wendy, was killed in a traffic accident. The hazy layers of fear, shock, sadness, loss and grief had to be unravelled. I quote her moving account at length:

> Our tears are for this earth only. God has given us this gift for now, not for later. Jesus said that part of His mission was to heal the broken-hearted and only He can take the tears and turn

our sadness into joy, as we have so painfully experienced.

I had to cope with Wendy's injuries and give her mouth-to-mouth resuscitation. I prayed. I talked to God, and I talked to Wendy with words of reassurance and love. Ambulance men and doctors took over, but she died a few minutes later.

My dilemma was how to cope with everyday life. Being a wife and a mother, doing the shopping and cooking, taking Suzanne (aged six) to school, while at the same time beginning to come to terms with the fact that I had had to save her life and I had almost been killed myself. Then I had to cope with Wendy's severe injuries and her death, the police and media interest, and the legal proceedings that were to last for almost six years.

I was broken. I didn't know that my emotions could be so strong. Shock, sadness, longing to hold Wendy, clean her teeth, brush her hair. I was torn inside with still wanting to care for her and to look after her. I had difficulty in allowing my maternal instincts towards her to end so abruptly. I was very aware of God, reaching down to me in Jesus, loving me and holding me, supporting me and caring for us as a family. Through all this I knew that I had to be real and not pretend.

The day of Wendy's thanksgiving service a

week later summed up in one day the sadness, shock, care and love that we all felt. I had found it easier to cry at night, to let go in the silence and the darkness. I didn't have to be strong for anyone and I could let go of the day's events. I went to bed the night before her service not knowing how I would manage the next day. It all seemed so unreal, to be attending the funeral of a young child. It was the wrong order of events. I expected to go to funeral services of elderly aunts and uncles, not my own daughter's.

Prayer for strength and courage came naturally. 'Lord, hold us, help us, may You be seen in all the circumstances.' I didn't know at the time that friends were staying up all night to pray for us. I wept silently and slept little. I must have fallen asleep eventually and awoke at dawn. My first conscious thought was that it was Wendy's service today. Then I realised that I wasn't crying.

I was aware of great peace in the bedroom and although the curtains were drawn everything seemed extra bright as if a spotlight was shining into the room. I felt a strong breeze which turned into a wind blowing over me. My hair was being blown, but the curtains didn't move. I knew something very wonderful was happening and I was very aware of the presence and closeness of Jesus. I didn't know what was happening, but as the wind blew over me my whole being was saying, 'Breathe on me breath of God. Fill me with life anew.' Over and over I repeated that prayer until the wind stopped. It wasn't until weeks later that I read in John 3:8 that the Holy Spirit was like a wind blowing, and no one knew where it came from or where it would go. For days, and all through the night, friends had been praying for our strength and comfort. God in His love had given us His Holy Spirit, the Comforter, to empower us and comfort us, to give us the strength and help we needed to get through each day.

So many people came to Wendy's thanksgiving service. Friends we knew and people we didn't know all came to share in our loss. Many were crying and we were able to comfort them. I stood and spoke about God giving us His Son so that we could have life. Suzanne and a little friend sang a song. Only God Himself could have given us the strength and energy to cope.

Later, at lunchtime, I remember my husband praying, 'Thank you, God, for giving us so much today', and then we both fell asleep in a chair for several hours! Such was our peace and exhaustion. That evening though, after we had put Suzanne to bed, all the events of the day caught up with us. We had been carried through, but now it was time to let go. I cried for two or three hours, letting go of shock, sadness and the strain of the day. It was like threads being snapped inside me. I just let go and cried and cried.

That really became the pattern all the way through. God holding us, reaching down to us, helping us while we had to go through formalities and then let go. I knew that I had to go through the pain and loss, to work through emotions that I didn't even know I had! I was physically and mentally exhausted. In the early stages just walking Suzanne to school and passing where Wendy died, four times a day, drained me. I had nothing left. Even common everyday events like going out and shutting the front door, or walking across a road, were a strain. I didn't know if I would reach the other side. I grew fearful.

It was at this time, when the initial shock was wearing off, that I felt the huge extent of my loss and overwhelming sadness. I wanted to let go but didn't know how to. I was afraid that if I really did then I would be totally out of control and that the tears would never stop. Also instead of forgetting the accident the police and solicitors wanted me to remember every detail for the courts! I had to begin to learn to remember without pain, to live without being emotionally disabled.

Because I felt so exhausted I didn't have the concentration to pray in any great detail, or to read my Bible. Yet I realised that Jesus was safe, solid, secure and that He cared about every detail in my life. After taking Suzanne to school I just simply went home to my bedroom. I lay flat on my bed and day after day simply said, 'I am here, Lord. Please minister to me.' It was the simplest act of submission. These were both painful and beautiful times. Each day would be different as I entrusted myself to the Holy Spirit. Sometimes I simply fell asleep and slept in peace, aware of God's presence with me. Often as I was lying down a particular hurt would come to the surface – the hurt needed facing, owning, feeling and releasing to Jesus. It wasn't easy. Sometimes the tears were almost silent, at other times like a torrid river. Deep sobbing as the pain was released, then healing, letting go, peace. Different hurts had to be given over time and time again – different facets of the same feelings and emotions. It wasn't self-pity or self-examination, rather a very hurting person handing over their life to God. I felt like a bathroom sponge full of water. Sometimes I would be gently squeezed and at other times it felt as if I was being wrung out. I knew that God was in control.

Often after the tears, a peace beyond measure would come and I would fall asleep or rest. Not only was I handing over the past and present, but also the shattered dreams and broken expectations of the future. The tears varied, quiet or strong, peaceful or burning, still tears and hurried tears tumbling over each other. It took time. I was aware of Jesus coming alongside sharing the pain with me, reaching down, holding, loving, healing. It was intimate and beautiful as well as painful. Jesus was setting me free and no detail was either too big or too small for Him. As I lay on my bed Jesus was reaching to me physically, mentally, emotionally and spiritually – in every aspect of my life – bringing comfort, love, healing and wholeness, giving me strength to live and love again. For me the tears were so important, a large part of that expression of sadness and fear, and later on of wonder and peace.

It took many years to work through the bereavement – far longer than I expected. I had to be patient. Most of it was alone with God.

The contrasts in this sad yet beautiful account from Eileen touched me deeply; the varied tears of bereavement so vividly expressing the loss of her precious child culminating in tears of wonder and peace. I must admit the challenge to me as I pictured Eileen lying on her bed, day after day, filled with utter pain and exhaustion, yet being able to say simply, 'I am here, Lord. Please help me.'

I thought of these words as Tom and I waited to visit a special friend in the Royal Marsden Hospital.

Julia had been suffering from cancer for almost six years and although we had only known her for three of those struggling years a deep bond and friendship had formed, mainly borne out of understanding the trauma of being a sick mother with two small children. Tim, Julia's husband, led us up to the ward and there was this beautiful, generous, loving happy brightness ensnared in a dying body. 'Please help me, Lord . . . please give me the right comfort and words.' Julia could not see us or speak but she held our hands tightly as she gasped each breath of life. Then I remembered the song that had been on my mind all day; I had been singing it for Julia as I thought about her and now it seemed the moment to sing it directly to her spirit.

> There is a Redeemer,
> Jesus, God's own Son,
> Precious Lamb of God, Messiah,
> Holy One.

> Thank you, O my Father,
> For giving us Your Son,
> And leaving Your Spirit —
> 'Til the work on earth is done.

> When I stand in Glory
> I will see His face.
> And there I'll serve my King for ever
> In that Holy Place.

This last verse I sang into her ear as she increased the squeeze of her puffy hand. It seemed that Julia knew then that she might be reaching heaven before the rest of us, although we did not know just how soon that might be. Of course her deep desire was to stay on earth to be Mum to her little boys, and wife, daughter and friend to so many people; yet this picture of Julia being in the Holy Place, looking into the face of the Redeemer as she served her King forever, brought great peace and even joy at that moment. We stayed just a little bit longer, silently praying and telling Julia how much we loved her and then we said 'Goodbye' for the time being. Julia died the following day.

The words of Eileen returned to me as I stood in the pew in a church packed with over five hundred people. I longed to wail, to weep *loudly* and really express my grief over Julia's suffering and death in a way that some people would say was not really becoming to an English woman. Tim and his young sons had just walked up the aisle and the service began, and so did my headache! 'Please help me, Lord' I prayed as my few remaining tissues became torn and shredded in their dampness. And then we sang 'There is a Redeemer'.

I couldn't sing. I choked. I coughed. I sniffed and blew. But no singing was possible, just an increasing thump and thud and pounding of headache. So this is grief, bereavement, loss. Tinged with the head knowledge that my dear friend was indeed in heaven, I had a heart full of sadness that only wanted to mourn.

'Please help me, Lord.'

Marilyn Baker got up and was led to the piano. Marilyn is blind yet she travels the world, giving concerts in which she sings the songs she has written and recorded. As she sat down to play, a peace descended on my spirit. Her words and clear voice were just like a soothing balm, and before she had finished singing my headache had completely disappeared. Marilyn had sung this particular song to Julia on her last day at home. I hope it will bring that same peace and 'soothing balm' as it is read, even without the melody:

Citizens of Heaven

Relaxing in the presence of Jesus
Resting in the shelter of His love,
Basking in acceptance and forgiveness,
Joined to our Father,
Citizens of heaven above.
Knowing He wants us close beside Him
Loved and chosen as His friends
So we've no need to fear,
With gladness we'll draw near to our Jesus
On whom our joy and hope depends.

Expressing grief in public, or rather suppressing grief in front of other people, can certainly lead to many

41

more problems than just a headache. Roy and Fiona Castle had the media watching their every move as they battled with Roy's cancer and then his death. Fiona soon realised that the aspirins she was taking to cope with headaches really were not needed when she allowed the unshed tears of grief to flow:

I don't shed tears easily. I suppose it is a throwback to the generation in which I grew up, during the war; I was taught to be brave and to endure. I also realised, from a young age, that I looked awful when I cried! Unlike my sister – whose eyes grew wide and big tears would spill over and roll down her cheeks – I screwed up my face, went rather purple and bawled. Not a pretty sight!

Tears, and in fact any display of emotions, were scorned at the boarding-school which I attended from the age of nine, so I very quickly learned to suppress my feelings. It is extraordinary to realise that even though I hardly ever cried through my own crises, I could weep buckets of tears in films and plays. I suppose I was projecting my emotions into other people's circumstances and imagining how they would be feeling. Tears are so therapeutic, and I certainly have known the release of emotions through tears in the past few years.

When Roy was first diagnosed as having lung cancer, the shock brought tears with it for the first twenty-four hours, until mind and emotions adjusted to the possibilities ahead of us. It was then that I realised, through watching my son struggling to keep his composure, that we had to give each other permission to express any emotions we might be feeling at any time. We did not need to be afraid of them, nor of other people's reactions to them; we were able to give each other space. This was a very valuable lesson to learn, which we carried through to Roy's death and beyond.

I developed a way of 'diverting' my tears at inopportune times and saving them for private moments. After a few weeks I realised I was occasionally taking aspirin for headaches. As soon as I allowed those unshed tears to flow, the headache disappeared.

Nine months after Roy died, I was sitting on a train reading a delightful book written by Susan Lenzkes called *Everybody's Breaking Pieces off of Me* (Discovery House, Grand Rapids, Michigan, 1992) – the way every mother must feel at times – and I read:

The God of all comfort cares for His hurting, weary children. He waits to hear our cry, waits to lift us out of the pit and hold us close to His heart. When He has nourished and strengthened us, then He will teach us how to walk in the calm as well as in the wind.

I wept. I wept tears of pain, of hurt, of weariness. The pain of separation was so acute, it might have happened only yesterday. Yet here was someone who was able to express in words what I could only feel. The tears flowed silently as I recognised my vulnerability and my weakness. How grateful I was for those 'everlasting arms' underneath me, to carry me and allow me to rest in Him. How glad I was too that there were very few people on the train!

A few weeks previously I was sensing the loss of a loving husband who would hug me and encourage me. The following morning I read *Living Light* for the day. This is what God had prepared for me:

Fear not; you will no longer live in shame. The shame of your youth and the sorrows of widowhood will be remembered no more, for your Creator will be your 'husband'. The Lord of Heaven's armies is his name; he is your Redeemer, the Holy One of Israel, the God of all the earth. (Isa. 54:4–5 Living Bible)

I wept. I wept tears of relief this time – relief that God understood my sorrows and my empty arms and through these verses He showed me that I never needed to feel lonely again. From now on

44

He would replace human love with His love.

> 'Before they call I will answer; while they
> are still speaking I will hear' (Isa. 65:24).
> God meets our every need and I have
> proved Him to be faithful to His promises.
> 'I will extend peace to her like a river . . .
> As a mother comforts her child, so will I
> comfort you' (Isa. 66:12–13).

Fiona Castle's son struggled to keep his composure when Roy's lung cancer was first diagnosed. In the same way, sixteen-year-old Rick battled with his grief. Rick already knew his little one-week-old sister was seriously ill with pneumonia and spinal meningitis when his parents returned home from the hospital.

> I guessed it was bad news the moment they
> walked through the front door. I saw the grief on
> Mum's face. I sat down and just stared off into
> nothing. Mum came over and put her arms
> around me and said, 'It's OK to cry, Rick. You
> don't have to be brave.' I wanted to cry but I
> couldn't. Don't get me wrong, I was full of
> emotion – anger, frustration, confusion, hurt,
> bitterness – but not full of tears.
>   At the funeral my whole family was crying
> and I still couldn't. The minister was crying, our
> friends and relatives were crying, and I just
> stood there. I knew people thought I was a hard

person. The tears just wouldn't come.

Later that afternoon, my grandmother came up and put her arms around me and told me she loved me. That was the first time I ever heard her say those words. Her face was stained with tears, her eyes were full of love and concern. And then I cried. It was such a relief to finally let the emotions go and the tears flow. That was the beginning of my getting over my sister's death.

The physical gesture of putting an arm around someone can often be the trigger to free the waves of emotions that build up. The absence of the touch of another human being can make suffering very lonesome and harder to bear. I always remember, as a child, when my parents ran a Sue Ryder home to give holidays to Polish survivors of concentration camps, how the Poles would hug us, pinch our cheeks and generally need physical contact to help in their terrific loss. Many had lost entire families in the holocaust and suffered terrible medical experiments and torture in the Nazi camps. Groups of about forty survivors at a time would arrive for a three-week stay to visit the sights of England.

Often, after supper, the group would assemble in the beautiful old drawing room of Stagenhoe Park. The elegance of the ceilings was not quite matched by the donated furniture and tired, understuffed sofas and armchairs. With coffee cups in hand, the Poles would begin to sing. Perhaps just one or two would quietly

start up a haunting melody. Gradually each one would
join in until the room was filled with such singing as
I have never heard before or since. It was explained to
us that this would have happened in the concentration
camps. Prisoners in one hut would begin to sing and
those in the next hut would join in until there was an
incredible, defiant song echoing from each hut.
Although the people were physically separated they
became joined as one as the singing spread through
the camp, and the guards appeared unable to stop it
happening.

As the Poles put down their empty coffee cups,
shut their eyes and lifted their faces upwards, I could
sense the awful memories mingled with their song. It
would not be too long before the handkerchiefs
appeared and silent, suffering tears flowed. I did not
really understand how, as a child, I could be of any
comfort to these brave survivors, but just sitting down
beside a quietly weeping bereaved mother and letting
her hug me seemed to be enough.

There is a moment before you cry when you can
check and stop what is about to happen. It is a sort of
'glug' feeling that sticks in your throat, yet if you try
to swallow it the unshed tears become a physical pain.
The body begins to count the cost and the spirit cries
out for comfort and compassion, not from Job's
comforters but from someone who will understand
what it means to mourn. The silent, loving friend who
passes the clean handkerchief is often the one who is
remembered as the person who best shared the grief.

The Blessing of Tears

As Jesus taught from the mountain, 'Blessed are those who mourn, for they will be comforted' (Matt. 5:4).

4

Big Boys Don't Cry

Let not women's weapons, water-drops,
Stain my man's cheeks!
    King Lear, William Shakespeare (1564–1616)

'Big boys don't cry' is a perfect summary of the stoical attitude our culture still fosters, especially among men. It often starts at school, where young boys learn successfully to freeze any emotional outlets.

Tom Benyon was told by the headmaster of one the country's most successful prep schools that he regarded it as his *prime* job to instil in his charges the need to *control* their emotions. Tom's reply to this headmaster was that he thought his skills would be most valuably deployed doing the exact opposite! The ethos of the school expected that boys should receive both bullying and punishment with no emotional display. To cry was to invite the further pain of ridicule. John Betjeman sums this up in his poem, 'Summoned by Bells':

Two other boys (my rivals, I suppose)
Came suddenly round a corner, caught my arms
And one, a treacherous, stocky little Scot,
Winded me with a punch and 'Want some more?'
He grunted when I couldn't speak for pain.
Why did he do it? Why that other boy,
Who hitherto had been a friend of mine,
Was his accomplice I could not divine,
Nor ever have done.

Let those who have such memories recollect
Their sinking dread of going back to school.
I well remember mine. I see again
The great headmaster's study lined with books
Where somewhere, in a corner, there were canes.

Experiences such as these shape the emotional lives of grown men. The boy-child quickly learns that his 'friends' will exploit any weakness or vulnerability and consequently adopts an emotional control. Wordsworth said, 'Shades of the prison-house begin to close upon the growing boy.' Before he can find a safe place in which to demonstrate these controlled emotions the constraints and demands of work and business take over. The world demands success and men are trained to perform. Competitive sport plays a part in this too (only nice guys come second!) and success is measured in the acquisition of money, attractive sexual partners, power and possessions.

A car sticker was spotted on a huge Cadillac in Manhattan that sums this up: 'He who dies with the most toys wins.' And so it is that many little boys grow up grabbing and grasping on to as many 'toys' as possible as they become steeped in the success syndrome.

But what happens to those feelings that have been locked into an emotional adolescence? Tom Benyon continues,

Any demonstration of vulnerability is taken as a sign of weakness, but of course vulnerability is a precondition of love. Unless you can share your thoughts, your hopes, your fears, your weakness and your need of God, how can intimacy flourish? Men are confused by a paradox which is that they believe vulnerability is weakness – as are displays of emotions, in particular crying. So they hide behind a shield of bravado. Men may go through the totem-pole dance of courtship and love, but in fact many have not grown up since they were shocked into an emotional ice-age when they were five years old.

Often you can watch a marriage break down as the wife leaves for another man. Often that man appears less handsome, less wealthy, and less successful in worldly terms, yet he is one who could love. The remaining husband appears to have no idea at all that his wife has been unhappy and it is as if their level of intimacy has never risen above the belt. They have never shared pain or joy, or love in its real sense, at any level other than the banal.

Some men suddenly find themselves staring helplessly at their own emotional apparatus that appears to have withered away. They cannot love. They have put 'things' in place of love. The void where love could be is now stuffed with materialism. Pascal said that there is a hole in every person's heart and it is God-shaped. If God does not fill it, then material things do.

If a man is unable to express himself emotionally, the currents of tears turn inwards and cause all sorts of havoc and sickness. Often men are aware of this dilemma but they are in the same hole as the man who listens to a Chopin Nocturne and is then presented with a piano and told to play! The music is familiar to him, but he cannot begin to perform it. He knows he is a mess and may identify with the poet Stevie Smith who wrote: 'I was . . . not waving but drowning.'

He knows he is fearful, inadequate and he has a bundle of the usual vices. He has been conditioned to think that if his wife and children knew what he was really like then they would cease to love him. So he 'pretends' all is well. The paradox is that his wife and children know what a silly old fool he is, and love him despite it! So men find tears *hard*. Women need to understand the dilemma and be gentle. It's not that men don't care. We do, dreadfully. It's just that we have been conditioned not to show it.

Royal Marines, and most service personnel, are not readily associated with showing emotion either. They certainly have been drilled not to show vulnerability or weakness. Often the job in hand needs emotional control and firm leadership. My older brother, Nigel Mumford, served a number of terms as a Royal Marine in Northern Ireland at the height of the troubles, but even after witnessing his friend being shot beside him he experienced few tears. Yet his experience of praying with a little child showed him how God longed to lift the bravado and conditioning and release the truth in him that big boys *do* cry. Nigel explains:

By a strange coincidence (or as I now call it, a 'Godincidence') I found myself in a pulpit for the first time, addressing about two hundred people. I had been asked to introduce Canon Jim Glennon from Australia during his visit to America for a particular week-long healing seminar.

I had not met Canon Glennon before, so I was

rather surprised, but nonetheless honoured, to be invited to do this task. My introduction was based on the healing of my sister, Julie, and the very real experience and effect this had on my life; of having seen her, so near to death, on the day before Canon Glennon's visit to pray for her, the day before Julie was healed.

As I stood up to speak I felt terrific heat in my spine. The heat was so intense that I feared the electrical outlet behind me in the pulpit was on fire. I turned around, to see nothing. I turned back and had the feeling of growth as my lungs filled and I grew taller, and with my head reaching up I let go of the lectern – no longer holding on to it for dear life!

My prepared speech went completely by the board and I have no idea what I said, but noted that instead of looking at the wall at the back of the church my head roamed up and down the pews looking into the eyes of every person there. Personally, I had been roaming too – right away from God for the past twenty years.

After the healing service, Holy Communion was to be offered. I found myself at the back of the church watching a few people leave, including a woman carrying a child. A moment later the same woman was standing beside me, her child snuggled into her neck.

As I was singing a hymn I thought she had returned to join in the singing, but she hadn't.

The woman was now in my space and moving to the front of me, looking directly into my eyes. Rather surprised, I asked her if she needed help. Her reply was simple. 'Will you pray for my child?'

I was quite astonished. I had prayed for myself a couple of times whilst in combat as a Royal Marine Commando and I had prayed for my sister, Julie, when she was sick, but I had never prayed for anyone else. For what seemed an age I did not know what to do or what to say. Suddenly I remembered my sister always asked the name of people who were requesting prayer so with relief I asked this lady, 'What is the name of your son?' 'Nicholas,' she replied. 'What is wrong with Nicholas?' I tentatively enquired. The mother proceeded to explain that her son was six years old and had been born with a misconnection in his brain. 'He cannot talk; he has no motor functions and cannot recognise anyone at all. He is basically a cabbage.'

I could not see Nicholas's face and I wondered, with increasing fear, how deformed his face must be. What a terrible thought that was. What do I do now? 'Help, God', I don't know what to do.

After a long pause I very gingerly put my hand on the boy's back. He was wearing a green down jacket and it felt quite thick, just right for the autumn as it was getting chilly outside. I only gently touched his jacket as I did not want to disturb him, for my own sake. What did this child look like, I wondered. Awful thoughts and images resembling the 'elephant man' flashed through my mind.

I began silently to pray for Nicholas. I prayed for his healing. I prayed that God might touch him and restore his brain. I also prayed for his mother and thought of the passage from the Bible about the woman who touched the hem of Jesus's cloak (Matt. 9:20–2). All the while I wondered why she had come to me when Canon Glennon was at this healing service. Again I prayed silently for Nicholas as I still did not want to disturb him (or was it because I had never prayed out loud!) and at the end of this simple prayer I just took my hand off his back. There was really no way that Nicholas could have felt this as I was so concerned about waking him. My touch had been so light yet as I lifted my hand away, Nicholas, as if in slow motion, pulled his head out of his mother's neck and turned his head towards me.

His eyes looked right into mine. He did not look around, he did not search, but looked right into my eyes, right into my soul. This beautiful looking child, with wonderful very large eyes, looked right into my soul. I have never been so moved in all my life. The tears fell from all four corners of my eyes. I had cried in my life but this was the first time that I had wept. Uncontrollable tears. Weeping, weeping.

I shall never forget the 'look' Nicholas gave me. It even makes me well-up writing about this now. Here was a child who seemed to know that he had been prayed for and he let me know it. How beautiful. How extraordinary.

I was the last person to receive Communion that night. I walked up the aisle with a very wet shirt and my head bowed. Jim Glennon said, 'Let's talk after the service' and this was my introduction to the healing ministry.

I do not know where Nicholas is. The rector of the church did not know his mother. I do not know where he is but I would love to see him again as I do often in my prayers. God bless you, Nicholas.

That experience with little Nicholas profoundly jolted my brother, Nigel, to reconsider his faith and has since led him to set up a Christian healing centre in Gaylordsville, Connecticut.

John Watson could not have imagined that something that happened to him at the age of ten could be relived, and healed, in his early forties. It surprised and encouraged him that at such an age he could be so deeply moved.

It began one evening, listening to a Radio 4 programme about an orphanage in Switzerland.

My wife, Lis, and I often listened to the radio in those days to take our minds off our respective working preoccupations. For some reason, listening to the orphaned children talking about their hopes for meeting their earthly parents in heaven one day moved me immediately to tears. It was very unusual for me at the time to behave in such a way, and thereafter I found I could become emotional 'at the drop of a hat' just by recalling the Radio 4 programme! But I could also 'switch off' the tears if I wanted to; they were in some way therapeutic and the experience was in no way threatening.

One day I decided to get to the bottom of what was behind all this. I felt that if I allowed myself to let the tears flow without stopping, I might find out. So one night, when I reckoned Lis was asleep, I 'turned on' the Radio 4 memory again, and let go. I don't remember how long I sobbed but my mind eventually turned to my own father, who had died when I was ten years old. I slowly began to appreciate, as I looked back, that I had still not finished with the grieving, or God with the healing of that memory, from this quite traumatic incident in my life. I had not gone to the funeral, which was not an unusual way of trying to protect children in those days. I remembered more my mother's grief, than my own, although others told me I had been quite distraught.

At the end of the sobbing I realised that I wanted to say that I loved my father, that I *really* loved him. I had never articulated this before and I felt I really wanted to do so, there and then. So I did, not out loud, but very loud and deep within my spirit. I told God that I loved *Him*, and felt much more able to handle that statement without getting angry with God for taking my father away from me.

And that was what it was all about: an experience that was part of freeing me from painful memories, of allowing me to express a deep love without pain at last, and then helping me to feel the pain in others whose loving relationships have unexpectedly and tragically been terminated. It was over thirty years later but I thank God that He can reach down and 'finish the business'.

These accounts from Nigel and John illustrate the very personal, but sometimes unlikely ways in which God can work in the lives of people, even after many years of apparent inactivity, or disinterest. It seems it is never too late. In totally unexpected and unlooked-for ways, God revealed something of Himself to these two men. Their emotions were deeply touched. For both Nigel and John, the outcome has been personal healing, and a ministry of Christian healing for others too.

In 1982 a book that filled many a Christmas

stocking was entitled *Real Men Don't Eat Quiche: A Guidebook to All that Is Truly Masculine* (by Bruce Feirstein, New English Library, 1982). Amazingly, we seem to have a rather dusty copy on the bookshelf! On the back cover the questions are asked, 'Are you a Real Man? Or are you puzzled, anxious, suffering from falling hair and loss of faith?' A quick dust down and flick through the pages revealed one or two interesting thoughts on men's perception of men!

Unlike his predecessors, today's Real Man actually can feel things like sorrow, pity, love, warmth, and sincerity; but he'd never be so vulnerable as to admit them . . .

When the dog dies, a Real Man breaks down and cries. He knows he could never bear to have another one . . .

When his wife dies, a Real Man remarries, knowing that that is what she would have wanted . . .

Only Quiche Eaters carry maps. Real Men *know* where they are – even when they're lost!

I chuckled at the hilarious, very tongue-in-cheek, descriptions of 'Real Men', but behind it all there was an element of truth! I'd also just been reading an article in the newspaper (*Daily Mail*, 25 January 1995) reporting on the Australian Open tennis tournament where a player would most certainly have been classed as a 'Quiche Eater' as he broke down and cried.

Touched by greatness and reduced to tears, Pete Sampras mounted perhaps the most dramatic recovery of recent tennis history to stay in the Australian Open. An innocent cry from the crowd at the end of a gripping fourth set had the Wimbledon champion in floods of tears. 'Win it for your coach!' was the exhortation that set Sampras weeping like a child in the heat of battle, serving at 1–1 in the decider.

Sampras composed himself, hurled down an ace, and after his head had bobbed into his towel at the next changeover he came out renewed and set about finishing the job. A full hour after the match Sampras was still almost too choked to speak, breaking down in front of the press.

And there it was. A full colour picture of Pete Sampras, racket in hand, with the caption: '"Break Point", Sampras's tears flow'. The press loved it. Perhaps it's just not true that 'Real Men don't cry' after all.

Many of the heroes on television, or in films, rarely, if ever, cry. The tough guy is always in charge of his emotions. If someone he loves gets hurt or killed, rather than grieve, he goes out to seek revenge. There are exceptions of course – Mel Gibson cried in *Lethal Weapon*, and Tom Hanks cried in *Forrest Gump*.

Rick always looked at his Dad as a 'Real Man' and remembered the first time he saw him cry:

> I was twelve years old, and two of my sisters had just died in a car accident. My dad came home from the hospital, put his arms around my sister and me, and just cried. He could barely get the words out that my sisters had died. I cried with him, not feeling a bit of shame, and it didn't shame me to see my dad cry either. It surprised me, though, because I always thought of my dad as really tough. He could do anything and he didn't show his emotions. And now he was crying. It showed me how much he cared. After that time I saw tears in my dad's eyes on many occasions.

It is a sad misconception to believe that real men should not show their emotions. However, real men do learn to control their emotions. Controlling one's emotions is a sign of emotional maturity – and it is the same for men and women. Controlling one's emotions is learning to recognise when one is angry, and deciding what to do with that anger; or feeling sad and choosing how to display that sadness. So a man who is emotionally mature knows when it's all right to show emotion – happiness, joy, surprise, fear, pain, hurt or sadness. He also knows when to cry. But it is too easy to be deceived into thinking that it is being manly or macho to hide ones emotions. Healthy emotional control does not include denying and suppressing feelings. That will only lead to greater emotional problems.

Actually, big boys do cry.

5

Moved to Tears

For some mysterious reason, I think I cry most when people win the Olympic Games. It seems like a lifetime of effort is rewarded. The rest of us must wait and see if we get a medal in heaven.

Alec McCowen

Although many people in Western cultures have been taught to hide their emotions, tears may be shed in all sorts of situations. Very often the words of a song or hymn can literally 'move us to tears', and those particular tears then can lead us on to something much deeper. David Edwards gives this example:

I had always believed that there was a God but never really knew who Jesus was. I remember well that a couple of weeks after reading my first Christian book – *My God Is Real*, by David

Watson – I found myself alone in my bedroom at college listening to a recording of the carol, 'O little town of Bethlehem'. I had the tape on as background music and I didn't think there could be much point in listening carefully to the words of a carol I knew so well from childhood. What happened next took me by surprise! Suddenly the words of the carol penetrated my heart.

> How silently, how silently, the wondrous
>   gift is given,
> So God imparts to human hearts the
>   blessing of His Heaven.

The magnitude of God's love, in giving Jesus for us, hit me in a way that I could not have conceived of before. Tears welled up inside me and began to pour down my cheeks. It seemed the more I wept, the deeper the sense of God's love touched me. It was as if the gate of my heart was opening up to delight in Jesus.

I seemed to be weeping tears of gratitude and tears of repentance for the way we had ignored Jesus. Tears of joy and sorrow flowed together. As I wept I felt God very near and I sensed a great weight lifting off my shoulders. It was a profoundly deep, enriching experience – one which provided a foundation for my early Christian life.

A good number of people testify to the impact music has had on their lives, and sometimes it is those 'old familiar words' that suddenly hit home. It is as if the stoppers have been removed from ears and the well-known words are heard as if for the first time, full of the deep meaning and passion that the writer intended.

I have my grandmother's old hymn-book. The pages are well worn and thumbed with a fragile, faded lace bookmarker placed between the pages of her special hymn.

> Breathe on me, breath of God,
> Fill me with life anew,
> That I may love what Thou dost love,
> And do what Thou wouldst do.

Inside the front cover of her hymn-book, my grandmother had listed her other favourites. I spent a glorious afternoon looking up each one and enjoying seeing and singing the words as though through my grandmother's eyes and ears. The hymns took on quite a different meaning and the impact of these words – because I believe my grandmother is now in heaven – filled me with such joy that I felt certain she was rejoicing with the angels!

On the next page were the words: 'Hark! hark, my soul! 223. My mother's favourite'. Quickly I turned the pages to find number 223, by F. W. Faber in *Hymns Ancient and Modern* (William Clowes and Sons, 1915):

Hark! Hark, my soul! Angelic songs are swelling
O'er earth's green fields, and ocean's wave-beat shore:
How sweet the truth those blessèd strains are telling
Of that new life when sin shall be no more.
Angels of Jesus, Angels of light,
Singing to welcome the pilgrims of the night!

Onward we go, for still we hear them singing,
'Come, weary souls, for Jesus bids you come':
And through the dark, its echoes sweetly ringing,
The music of the Gospel leads us home.
Angels of Jesus, Angels of light,
Singing to welcome the pilgrims of the night!

Far, far away, like bells at evening pealing,
The voice of Jesus sounds o'er land and sea,
And laden souls, by thousands meekly stealing,
Kind Shepherd, turn their weary steps to Thee.
Angels of Jesus, Angels of light,
Singing to welcome the pilgrims of the night!

Rest comes at length; though life be long and dreary,
The day must dawn, and darksome night be past;
Faith's journey ends in welcome to the weary,
And Heav'n, the heart's true home, will come at last.
Angels of Jesus, Angels of light,
Singing to welcome the pilgrims of the night!

Angels! sing on, your faithful watches keeping,

Sing us sweet fragments of the songs above;
Till morning's joy shall end the night of weeping,
And life's long shadows break in cloudless love.
Angels of Jesus, Angels of light,
Singing to welcome the pilgrims of the night!
Amen.

By the time I had finished singing this one, the tears
were gently coursing down my cheeks as I could just
picture my grandmother and great-grandmother at
their 'heart's true home' surrounded by 'cloudless
love' and singing their hearts out as they too welcome
the pilgrims of the night! A tiny scrap of paper
suddenly fell out of the old hymn-book. I recognised
the handwriting. My grandmother had written, 'I
think when I read that sweet story of old; when Jesus
was on earth among men, How I wish I had been with
Him then.' This sounds as if it might also be from a
hymn. As I looked at these words, I almost felt as
though I'd intruded on something very intimate, and I
wondered whether it was the words of this hymn-book
that had spoken to her heart in such a way that she had
decided to be baptised and confirmed at the age of
seventy.

My tears were not prompted only by the moving
words of the hymn, but also by our family memories
of my grandmother's death. Her daughter, my mother,
described in her journal the minutes from 12 noon
to 12.05 p.m. on 16 February 1991.

It was *the look*. The physical 'look' of the human
spirit, combined with the Holy Spirit, looking
on Almighty God. It was the moment of meeting, and I saw it. It was a few moments of utter
wonder, peace, glory, holiness. It was looking
into heaven. Looking into the kingdom of
God. Looking *at* God. No breath was needed.
No breath came, just supreme wonderment.
The glory of God in His heaven *shone* in her
blue, bright renewed eyes. The glory was seen
reflected in her eyes. She looked beyond this
earth; beyond me, the room, the building – into
the presence of God – Father, Son and Holy
Spirit – and to them she went. I am quite sure.
The body wasn't needed any more. Spirit was
reunited with spirit.

Faith's journey ends in welcome to the weary,
And Heav'n, the heart's true home, will come at
    last.
Angels of Jesus, Angels of light,
Singing to welcome the pilgrims of the night!

Music, and the words of songs and hymns, can often
reach into the depths of the soul in ways that have a
healing effect. Marion Cripps, who suffers with
multiple sclerosis, went to stay at Burrswood – which
is a Christian centre for medical and spiritual care in
Kent – where she received much care and counselling.
It appeared that nothing that was said to help her,

regarding coming to terms with the illness, seemed to work, until one day she was given a music tape.

> I listened to the songs but was really struck by one in particular. It was about water washing over you, cleansing and healing as it flowed. As it was sung I just wept buckets of tears. I kept on playing it, perhaps three or four times a day for a fortnight, and each time I experienced the healing waters of Jesus washing over me, cleansing and healing me. I cried each time it was sung and gradually the inner healing came until by the end of my stay at Burrswood, the weeping had stopped and I could listen to the song without crying.

The words of another hymn:

> Give Him all your tears and sadness
> Give Him all your years of pain,
> And you'll enter into life in Jesus's name

brought real meaning to Drina Chalmers after a lifetime of grief and loss of her family. When she was a young girl she saw her grandfather die in his armchair, her mother committed suicide and her brother drowned at the age of fourteen. 'I soon began to enclose myself in a "block of ice". No one could hurt me there. Over the years I thawed a little, married and had four children, but was often told I lacked compassion as I was so unsympathetic towards people who cried.'

There followed years of illness and then Drina's husband suddenly dropped dead. Her daughters took her to their church where she made a commitment to follow Jesus.

> Afterwards we sang this lovely hymn. The words were so beautiful that I found myself crying, because the words were speaking directly to me. It was as if the block of ice was at last melting. This led to my being baptised and when asked to give a reason for coming to baptism I said, 'I have learnt to cry again.' I remembered then that Jesus wept.

Apart from music and songs, there are numerous occasions that reduce people to tears. My daughters often complain to me, 'Oh, Mum, you're so emotional. It's embarrassing!' I can cry soppy tears even when watching the advertisements on television. (I felt much better when a friend said she cried watching *Blue Peter*!) Tom, my husband, says I'm a nightmare to take to the cinema as I cry just as much in the happy films as the sad ones. I have only to hear the first few notes of the wedding march, or 'Here comes the bride', and that's me gone! To see a couple at the altar, looking into each other's eyes as they repeat their vows, can have many reaching and fumbling for handkerchiefs.

Practical love in action can move people to tears. Acts of gentleness and compassion; the tender caring of one human being for another; thoughtful, appropriate help can moisten the eyes of onlookers. Many people cry for the plight of animals in distress through cruelty or neglect. It is so often vulnerability that appeals to our emotions – whether in people, animals or situations.

Mary Fisher, a breeder of Afghan hounds, told me how watching Crufts dog show brings tears to her eyes. I was intrigued and asked her to explain further.

It's the obedience class that really does it. The way the dogs watch every move and signal from their master or mistress. The way the dogs seem to sense what the handler requires of them. They're so 'in tune' with one another. It makes me want to cry because the dog is so utterly trusting, yet watchful and alert for any change in direction or command. With each signal the dog is longing to please his master. You can see it in their eyes.

The discipline of listening to God, and the outcome at times, are things that have often moved me to tears. I once was getting ready to go and speak at a healing service in America when I almost 'heard' an audible voice telling me to do something very simple. I had just finished getting dressed and was about to leave the bedroom when I had an urge to return to the dressing table and put on a string of beads. 'No,' I told myself as I held them up to the front of my dress, 'They're a bit "over the top"! They would look much better for an evening occasion' and I went to put them back in the box. 'Put on the beads . . .' I turned around sharply thinking someone was in the bedroom with me, and then I 'heard' it again. 'Put on the beads.' It sounded so authoritative. Not harsh but just a command that you wouldn't argue with. I found myself saying out aloud, 'Yes, of course!'

During the car journey to the church I felt somewhat over-dressed with these beads but soon put it out of my head as we arrived for the morning service. A young mother brought her child to the rail for prayer. She explained that her little daughter was two years old and was very sick indeed. Genetically all sorts of things were wrong with the tiny child so her development, walking and speech were all impaired. Her mum was distraught as she spoke to us, but faithfully felt she should bring her child forward for prayer. It was extremely difficult to hear or pray as this little one could certainly make a great deal of noise! Her wailing and screams soon were matched by the young mother who was exhausted and unable to comfort her child.

'Of course! The beads.' The words flashed through my mind so quickly I was almost taking the string of beads off before I realised what I was doing! I handed them to the little girl, and immediately she was quiet and still. We could all see how much she enjoyed the feel and texture of the beads, and straight away she put them into her mouth. And then we prayed.

My husband Tom looked up from where he and I were kneeling with the mother and child to see the entire church – the whole congregation – with their arms outstretched in prayer towards the mother and her baby. All those people, with their own problems and sicknesses, were sharing the moment of compassion and pain, as if corporately lifting the mother and daughter up into the presence of Almighty God.

That little example began to teach me how to listen to that 'voice' behind you, saying, 'This is the way; walk in it' (Isa. 30:21). Sometimes I get it very wrong but I am beginning to trust that voice. A song that I often use as a prayer, has helped this 'listening'.

O give me a hearing heart, O Lord
Give me the will to obey.
Give me a desire to renew my love
To keep my heart open through the day.
And give me a holy fear, O Lord,
Give me a hatred of sin.
Cleanse me from secret and shameful thoughts,
Brighten the eyes that have grown dim.

That I may see, that I may hear,
That I may love the things that you hold dear.
That I may change, that I may grow,
That your likeness may now begin to show.
Give me a hearing heart,

The Blessing of Tears

Give me a hearing heart,
Give me a hearing, hearing heart.

And give me a faithful heart, O Lord,
Give me the nerve to believe.
You give me the confidence to draw near,
Freedom to come and receive.
And give me a waiting heart, O Lord,
To stay silent before your throne.
Give me a real and determined desire,
To seek you and serve you alone.

There are occasions when the situation is almost too awful for tears at all. I admit to being emotionally numb sometimes in the past, when watching the news on television. It often came on just as we finished eating our supper. Faced with appalling pictures from war-torn countries, or of devastating famine, it was if I simply could not take in what was being shown. That changed, quite dramatically, for me after meeting up with a friend, Alli Blair, who had returned home for a three-week break after working in Rwanda in Africa from the end of the civil war in 1994.

We sat on the sofa, and I had a mug of tea in one hand and the other hand cupped over my mouth, stifling gasps of terror. Alli had taken a number of photographs and as she turned the pages of the album the horror of the life she had come from began to unfurl. Alli's job in Rwanda was to be the project manager for a centre for unaccompanied children.

This was not really an orphanage as many of the children had parents still alive, but they had been separated during the raids on villages, and long processions to refugee camps. Mainly Alli's work was to trace any members of a child's family who might still be alive, and reunite them.

Occasionally there shone out from the photographs a little face, reunited with an aunt or grandmother. Very rarely, it seemed, was it with a mother. Then she showed us the 'before and after' pictures of emaciated little bodies looking so scared and lost. The expression sprang to my mind, 'It looks as if they've seen a ghost.' But of course it was not ghosts these children had seen, but the brutal murder of their parents and their brothers and sisters. Many had witnessed a child hacking another child to death.

As Alli recounted tale after tale I had to ask: 'Is there anything good happening there?' The images of suffering were becoming too much for me to bear. She stopped for some while to think, and took a sip of tea. But she did not answer my question, not straight away.

Alli is an experienced aid worker, having spent eight years on the Thai/Cambodian border, and five years inside Cambodia, working with refugees from the Pol Pot regime who had also witnessed fearful incidences of barbarism and killing. But of course she had also seen, in the middle of immense suffering, much courage and her stories of reconciliation and love shown within those refugee camps were good to listen to. But now she seemed reticent, and unable to put her thoughts beyond the horror shown in these photographs.

To break the tension I found myself laughing at a picture of Alli in her tent sitting up in her camp bed, with a big broad grin for the camera. Beside her camp bed was an object like a brief-case.

'Alli, what's that for?'

'Oh, that's my light! In the morning I take it outside and leave it in the sun all day. Then in the evening, when I return, I bring it into the tent and there is light! You see, it's a solar lamp.'

I could see she was still thinking about my question. Then Alli said,

The thing is, if you look at the situation as a whole, it is hopeless. But if you take each child, deal with each one separately, and just do as much as you can, then you do see good. Sometimes you take one child, and not another. You pick out a baby rather than a toddler; the decisions are awful. The scale of suffering is out of our control. When I return to the tent at night, I pick up my solar lamp and it brings light into the darkness. And then I need to spend some time, sometimes weeping, but usually I'm just too tired . . . but I need to spend time basking in God's light, asking for strength and courage, and wisdom for those difficult decisions. I suppose it's a bit like being recharged with 'heavenly sunshine'! But if I don't do it I'm not sure I'd be able to step outside that tent in the morning.

Alli returned to Rwanda soon after this and it was on receiving a copy of her diary that I really wept.

Alli Blair's Rwandan Diary 1995

Tuesday 18th April:

All food distribution due to stop in remaining southern camps.

Thursday 20th April:

Awful, choking evil dream last night. Long, strange, complex and occult – not simply a nightmare. Second time only in my life that I remember such a vivid experience of evil.

Pray for those dying in the camps. No food, no water, no medical care, cold rain, no sanitation – potential dynamite. Many casualties in a stampede involving bullets, clubs, machetes and bayonets. By 7 p.m. twelve reported dead, twenty-three wounded.

Friday 21st April:

Keep me   in praise positive
             in decisions compassionate
             in attitude gracious
             in hope faithful
             in prayer without ceasing
             in wisdom dependent on You.

Saturday 22nd April:

Kibeho. Fifth day with no food. Hunger, sickness, fear, menace, men treating other human beings as animals, gratuitous revenge killings in thin disguise. Self-defence, of course. Hopeless, helpless targets. Some guilty, most innocent. Women, children, babies, sick and elderly caught in nightmare soulless trap. Chaos, insanity. Twenty-three killed and close to sixty badly injured. (This figure swells to an estimated five thousand dead and countless disappeared over the following days.)

The world looks on and sees it simply as 'more ethnic unrest'. Non-governmental organisations look on, hands tied. UNAMIR watches in horror, also forbidden to take any action. A captain friend describes what he sees and weeps. I searched for words to speak into his deep despair and I was numb before the horror and mystery of the slaughter still going on now, as I write.

They have become filled with every kind of

wickedness, evil, greed and depravity. They are full of envy, murder, strife, deceit and malice . . . God-haters, insolent, arrogant and boastful; they invent ways of doing evil . . . they are senseless, faithless, heartless, ruthless (Rom. 1:29–31).

Is there no other way? Should we all go home now and let history wreak its inevitable revenge in the present without ignorant interference from outside which only aggravates? What are you saying to us, Abba? Or are you showing us naked evil, naked helplessness, and trying to remind us of our own ignorance and impotence?

No 'saviour mentality' arrogance can stand in the face of this insanity. My soul aches, my reason is nauseated, my mind refuses to rest before the magnitude of gross inhumanity and insists on understanding yet without success. My body, my strength, wants to be heroic, active, fling itself down or climb to the heights for the sake of peace and justice, but instead I continue in my little corner – fretting instead of praying.

And my spirit. My spirit is deeply disturbed although my faith is unshaken. Somehow God is big enough to encompass the reality that I want to deny. I don't need to help Him be God just because Rwanda doesn't fit my theology.

Lord, accept this inner turmoil as a prayer offering on Your altar. Guide me through the struggle and help me to use the tools and weapons You are offering to meet my needs. Don't allow me to add an imported anger, hatred and bitterness to a situation already seething putrid with such evil. When You call may I be ready to respond but don't let me stray outside Your will just to indulge myself or impress my neighbour.

Sunday 23rd April:

Rain, cold, pee, poo, dysentery, pain, infected wounds, festering corpses, terror, threats, insults, fear, anger. Bullets, machetes, barbed wire, brutal beatings, hunger, thirst, sickness, smell, despair. Evil, evil, evil.

Misha and Sergei drop in to de-brief. Hardened Russian submariner, Misha has just returned from Kibeho freaked out. Normally jocular and irrepressible, the two 'Milobs' (Military Observers) are shocked and sober. Sergei helps Misha sensitively with some of the more difficult vocabulary he needs and I help Sergei with one or two words. As a tribute to the seriousness of the occasion we break all traditions and drink only water. As if in a dream Misha tells of the bodies, the bayonets, the decapitated babies, the woman who in fright, reached down to scoop water from a dirty rivulet, was surrounded and beaten to death in front of him.

Thursday 27th April:

Rain. Meetings. 2.30 p.m. Butare Feed the Children
Transit Centre rendezvous with social workers and big
white truck which will carry thirty-nine children to
Gikongoro. Dark eyes, cheeky faces, scared faces,
winces from the many with foot wounds as they are
helped aboard. How I'd love to travel with them but I
must provide the escort.

I pray, just repeating the name of Jesus and appeal
to every angel within earshot. Don't let the children be
freaked out by an armed search and interrogation,
after all they have been through. Suddenly God
reminds me that He is in control and they are His
children and just relax and trust. I relax a muscle or
two.

We arrive in brilliant sunlight. The access is too
muddy so the truck gets stuck and we unload above
the school before a growing crowd of curious
onlookers. Blue sky, splat mud landing. I enjoy the
trust hug as little ones leap into my arms extra-
ordinarily trusting, not knowing where they are except
that it is a long way from the horror of Kibeho.

A song of welcome by the 'old' children is inter-
rupted by shrieks of joy from Fidele who has found
his brother Samuel, and the two dance around in an
ecstatic embrace as all the others cheer. My eyes fill
yet again.

Friday 28th April:

Irrationally I want the rest of the world to cease all normal activities to mourn and intercede for Rwanda, while here I long to see signs of normal activities which comfort my soul – a woman hoeing, a shepherd waif waving, 'Komera!' (Courage!), a home-made wooden scooter-bike careering down the hillside with a load of potatoes.

Whilst I sit and write or eat or read, while I fill my hot water bottle and pull six blankets over me at night, an alternative reality plays in Kibeho. No food, no drink, no blankets, no comfort, no respite. 'Twas ever thus. Throughout my life horror stories have been unfolding while I play, and normally how easy it is to blot out the voice whispering of other's misery, compared to my plenty. Can I still be in doubt as to how to respond after so many years of being aware of the paradox? Suddenly when it's in my back yard I cannot avoid it.

If we are all one in God then when one suffers we all suffer, whether we feel it immediately or not. Alleviation of the other's suffering is actually balm to my own body if I could only understand this biblical truth. Think globally, yes, but do act locally. Yes, I am my brother's keeper if I would want him to do the same for me in time of affliction.

Saturday 29th April:

As we come closer to pain's epicentres and human suffering so we come closer to the cross. The veil was rent in two long ago but the further we remove ourselves from the suffering of others, the more substantial the veil over our understanding of the crucifixion love. My desire to seek God has instinctively led me, reluctantly, to frontiers of human suffering which naturally I would choose to avoid, longing to understand how He, who is love, can be right there amidst the most chronic grotesque manifestations of hate. But of course it is the obvious place to find Him, exposed on the cross. The veil over understanding comes with the distancing from the pain. Not that I can even claim the right to understand. I can neither experience nor offer Christ's love until I make myself as vulnerable as He did physically, emotionally, letting go of all mechanisms for self-preservation. Concern for my physical safety and concern for my heart, my image must go. It is only in the breaking of the vial of perfume nard that the fragrance is released to delight others. So with us – we must be broken to release what is valuable.

Monday 1st May:

Now it's May Day!

On Wednesday I was interviewed at the centre for unaccompanied children and filmed for World Vision, mainly Canada. When asked at the end how I personally was dealing with all that was happening, I suddenly collapsed in tears, on camera, of course, so you can imagine how thrilled they were! I don't care, we hugged a lot afterwards and it was a good relax. Emotions closer to the surface than I had realised.

Allison witnessed the effects of civil war on children and communities. Her diary entries record events, and her struggles to come to terms with them. This process included tears for her at the time, and may continue to do so for those who read her words.

Of such tears, which may *seem* insignificant, Dr James Fleming says,

> Our little tears, if enough people cry, become a stream, that turns into a river, that heals the land. Because what we cry about we talk about, and what we talk about we act upon.

6

Healing from Inside Out

Every tear that should have been shed
adds another drop to my reservoir bed.
The level climbs up the wall of the dam,
not facing up to who I really am.

The pressure is on, the edges erode.
Where can I go with this heavy load?
The bricks start to crack, the wall's nearly lost.
My body is starting to count the cost.

Pour forth, river of tears; break free from your
*   snare.*
Flow to your maker who's longing to care.
Drain every drop that lies captive within.
Fill up that pool with an assurance of Him.

Anna

It was an enormous shock when, having been a ballet

dancer and totally in control of all my muscles, I found myself struck down by a neurological illness that left those trained muscles completely out of control. Bed pans, being spoon-fed, bathed and dressed are the best removers of the performer's mask I know of! I had contracted the generalised form of the neurological movement disorder called dystonia, having been married for seven years with two daughters then aged one and three.

With increasing disability and decreasing hope of ever walking again (or more importantly being able to care for our children), it began to feel as if my faith in God was being tested by the burning and scorching flames of the refiner's fire. The pain of the muscle spasms alone brought days and nights of torment. The emotional strain of being stared at, because of the strange contortions my limbs went into, certainly did not give me a positive body image! I was used to being the ballet dancer, looked at for beautiful movements. This was different entirely. Often, first-time meetings were tinged with the assumption that I wasn't quite 'all there', and in many ways this led to another mask being worn as I endeavoured to appear 'normal'. I covered up my emotions.

As a dancer, I had portrayed joy and freedom, often concealing intense physical pain. I continued this act when I was actually desperately ill. I disguised the depths and reality of my pain, partly from fear of being called hysterical by members of the medical profession. They were having difficulty in diagnosing my condition, and when it did not respond to or indeed worsened after their attempts to treat me, the possibility that my illness had an emotional rather than a physiological basis was investigated.

As the weeks of disability and pain lengthened into months, I feared that my friends would stop visiting me. But the more outwardly unlovely I became, the more effort it took for me to appear positive and welcoming for the sake of others. If sick people start slipping down into the slough of despond, the label 'depressed' is quickly attached to them, and personally I dreaded this particular tag.

I shed tears, of course, as bit by bit my 'ballerina body' packed up, but often these tears were cried alone at night under the hospital bedcovers. When the children came to visit, a slightly false air of normality was adopted. I'm sure we reinforced that 'war child' attitude of 'being brave and not crying', especially when it came to being separated again at the end of visiting time. We were really just pretending and buoying one another up until that time we all hoped for, when Mummy would be better again – when our own personal world war would be over.

Looking back, I can see that my healing was accompanied by many tears. Crying was part of the healing process for me, although I did not realise it so clearly at the time. (My first book, *Dancer off her Feet*, published by Hodder and Stoughton in 1991, gives an account of the illness and healing.)

My uncle, Alec McCowen, took on the incredible feat of learning the entire Gospel of St Mark and then spent a number of years reciting this in theatres and churches throughout the world. A few verses that moved him greatly come in Mark 9, and I remember hearing this in a new way when he said it. Perhaps the old words of the King James version helped! Alec recalls:

> A distraught father brings his son to be cured, but is disappointed when the disciples are unable to do it. Then Jesus arrives and begins to cross-question the father, telling him harshly, 'If thou canst believe, all things are possible to him that believeth.' And then we hear an echo of every family when a loved one is sick – an echo heard at one time for you, Julie – 'And straightway the father of the child cried out, and said with *tears*, "Lord, I believe; help thou mine unbelief." '

That desperation in the father's cry is familiar to many people as they face their own, or another person's, illness and suffering. Beth Ellis worked among barefoot street children in Beira, Mozambique. After years of civil war leaving families torn apart, the children had learnt to fend for themselves on the streets, coping with daily abuse by stealing and begging. Most were HIV-positive. Dirty, cheeky, vulnerable and hungry for love, these youngsters could 'give' even though they had so little.

One night we gathered to pray for one of the
team who, due to an incorrect prescription of
malaria pills, had become seriously debilitated
and close to despair without the essential
medical attention he needed. The door was flung
open and two of the resident staff stood there
alongside four of the youngest street boys. 'The
boys want to pray for Chris, too.' I held out my
hand to encourage them into the room and they
squeezed on to the bed. We started to pray again,
laying hands on the ailing Chris, asking for
God's healing and peace. One after the other the
prayers came and then the little husky voice of
Dje. This eight-year-old, with no family of his
own, began to pray earnestly and passionately in
Portuguese: 'Jesus, Senhor. Please heal our
Christopher who teaches us football. Please
Jesus, Senhor.'

I started weeping unashamedly, tears streaming down my cheeks and all over Dje's fuzzy
little head. Then Constantin took up the prayer,
equally passionately, followed by Jeremias.
These little rejects – flotsam and jetsam, African
equivalents of Dickens' nineteenth-century
London street urchins in *Oliver Twist* – prayed
without doubting in their hearts that Senhor
Jesus would heal their football coach. I knew at
that moment that Jesus was indeed with us as

that room filled with His love and peace. As if
to help any 'unbelief', the door opened and the
youngest member of the team, nineteen-year-old
Sarah, came in with a saucer of oil, saying she
felt we should anoint Christopher, and as she
knelt to do so the telephone rang. It was a
mission doctor ringing to speak to Christopher
after many weeks of waiting for him to call.

This story is all the more poignant because Beth
herself lost her own son when he was tragically
murdered.

A few weeks after the funeral, I felt I should go
to the church my son had attended, really only
out of politeness to the curate who had looked
after all the arrangements and our emotional
needs with great sensitivity. Once there, I was
surprised when the young people in front of me
raised their arms while singing, and suddenly I
was in floods of tears. I continued to return to
this church and each time the tears just flowed. I
asked the curate what on earth was the matter
with me. To my wonder, he said, 'I believe you
are being powerfully blessed by the Holy Spirit,
Beth', and more tears flowed! 'Me?' Six years
later I am still wonderfully blessed, and want to
reassure people of the validity and healing
power of tears.

When we hear the word 'healing', it often makes us think of being physically well and whole, whereas I'm sure that God's idea of healing is much greater than that. It seems as if we very often need to be healed from the inside, and then outwardly, and the external tears are the first sign of healing taking place internally. From many Christian traditions we have inherited the man-made requirement to radiate victory and joy and assurance. These qualities should indeed radiate from Christians, but when they do not too often believers have been forced to wear the plastic smile in order to be loved and accepted. The Holy Spirit leads us into all truth and sooner or later He will face us with ourselves as we are.

Pam Fardon attended a week's residential conference, and as Agnes Sandford rose to speak at the first session, to an audience of mainly men, a thought flashed through Pam's mind: 'I need to be broken and put together again.' 'Please do it, Lord,' Pam whispered.

I listened to Agnes with rapt attention. There was nothing emotional in any of the remarkable stories she told, yet I wept. Time and time again I bowed my head and wiped my tear-stained face. I am a person who looks red-eyed and awful when I cry, but when I escaped to look in a mirror my face looked completely normal. The tears continued. They seemed like a constant flow of gentle water washing the rubbish away. I felt very weak and very vulnerable, but I sensed a voice in my head gently reassuring me. 'I'm finished for now.'

Caroline also experienced tears healing her inside out. She had spent a number of church meetings sitting at the back crying and said,

> Although some were 'feeling sorry for myself' tears, most were tears of wonder at this God I was hearing about. This led to a definite commitment to Christ. As I was being prayed for on another occasion I felt as if my spirit had been broken and that there had been a spiritual release. I sensed a very real healing from God for my crushed spirit as He took the hurt and rejection, and gave me a sense of 'coming home'.

The sense of frustration and the need to express what is truly going on inside is poignantly recorded by a friend I trained with at ballet school. Sarah Scott, daughter of the comedian Terry Scott, went on to be an actress and performer specialising in 'sign song'. This is a deeply expressive form of interpretation of songs through dance with sign language for those who cannot hear the music. Sarah herself has been partially deaf all her life.

Tears

At school

First school,
a tug of war at five years old.
Hearing aid.
Asthma, eczema, a broken collar
bone . . .
So *why* did Mum have to leave me?

At bedtime

At boarding school
lights out.
The others are chatting
but my hearing aid is out . . .
What are they talking about?
Is it about me? . . .

School desk

I can't hear, I can't hear,
I can't hear what she's saying.
I don't know what's to be done.
I daren't ask.
I daren't show myself up,
Make me look stupid . . .

The doctors

So many things to explain.
So many ailments.
I'm not making it up.
I'm not a *deaf fool*.
It's all so very personal
All welling up in me . . .

The Blessing of Tears

Frustration   Pushing and pushing.
My body won't work.
I hate myself for its failures.
I have to succeed.
I have no choice and the release
when I have made the breakthrough
shows in my eyes.

Music   It's sheer perfection.
Now I know what
pulling at your heart strings really
means.

On stage   All my 'rubbish',
all expression swells in my chest
and explodes in my eyes
and through my body
as I use sign language and
dance . . .

Pain   Mum's pain.
Dad's pain.
I wish I could save them from it,
protect them.
It's a kind of agony.

Grief   Dad . . .
His soul leaving
as the drugs and disease take over.
The pain is so deep and hard inside.

I still can't believe it.
I was there . . .
I saw him go . . .
but I can't believe
he's actually gone . . .

In God's House Welling up.
Reaching.
Look up to the heights.
So much suppressed emotion.
And this is one person
Who *knows* I can't lie
or pretend . . .
It all comes up . . .
Is that why I shy away?

Shirley Buckner speaks for many people when she
describes her experience:

There had been much rejection, failure, lack of
love, lack of self-esteem and poor self-image
from the womb to the present. Each time God,
by His Holy Spirit, brings up an area He is going
to deal with there will be many tears from me,
as He first releases and then heals the various
emotions which have been locked away for
many years. There was a time, for about three
years, when I would be in tears at every meeting
I attended. It was not possible for me to be in
God's presence and not cry, so deep were the

hurts and so persistent His ministry to me. Weeping has become more rare now that the bulk of my past has been dealt with. Psalm 56:8 speaks of our tears being recorded in God's book and that made me realise that He knew everything that had happened, and that He cared when no one else did.

To be brought up in a legalistic church in North East Scotland meant that the 'stiff upper lip' was the way in which everything was met – joy and sorrow, ecstasy or tragedy. Anne recalls living through a war and very rarely seeing anyone in tears. As for weeping in church, it would have been regarded as a sign of a lack of spiritual maturity.

The result of this was that by the time I grew up and married the only thing that ever produced tears in me was sheer rage. As I am an equable person, seldom losing my temper, tears were a rarity in our home! Even a serious illness shortly after we were married was lived through with a very real sense of God's presence but not one tear, except tears of exhaustion which had no emotional content. Once the illness had been properly diagnosed and treated, the news that we would probably never have children, and the subsequent arrival of our two 'miracle' daughters, brought immense joy but again there were no tears.

Then God began to work in what I thought was a very strange way. I suddenly discovered that I could no longer speak about the love of God and Jesus's death without tears. How embarrassed I was at what I thought of as weakness! Then I found myself in tears during a communion service and thought the rebuke I received from the wife of one of the elders richly deserved. But it happened on more than one occasion and God began to show me that this was nothing to be ashamed of. After all He had wept for me.

In a new church, almost every Sunday morning during worship and invariably at communion I found myself in floods of tears. I began to take several large hankies to every service, and they always came home sodden. I was convinced that everyone would think I had developed water on the brain!

I began to feel compelled by God to speak in the open worship time during the service. Again I was so ashamed to find my voice cracking and floods of tears flowing until someone pointed out to me that my tears and joy of my worship were releasing others. Shortly after this I had my first conscious experience of being filled with the Holy Spirit and found myself dancing around the kitchen, tears streaming and shouting praise at the top of my voice! (I had never been able to dance – another legacy of my upbringing.) Since then I have learned to welcome the tears and see that God uses them, not only for my healing and release, but to release others. On a number of occasions I have found myself sobbing from the very core of my spirit and these have been times of tremendous healing when so many of the buried fears and hurts of my childhood and early adulthood have been dealt with. During this present wave of the Holy Spirit's blessing I have twice found myself on the floor with enormous sobs shaking me with a tremendous sense of God's love pouring into me. My prayer is: 'More, Lord'.

As God changes us and softens our hearts from the inside out, it becomes impossible to keep that transformation and healing of our hard heart to ourselves. His love pours into our hearts and we then pass it on! Stefanie experienced this soon after she became a Christian.

Every time I went into church, sang a hymn or prayed the tears just poured out. I was very aware of the 'melting' of my hard heart. I had pushed God out for so long and built a barrier in my heart. I became aware of standing naked before God and was so relieved that with Him I didn't have to try to be anything other than me. I knew He could see right into my very being yet He still loved me. Then as He broke me, melted

me and moulded me I became so aware of other
people who needed His love. Songs like 'Make
me a channel of your peace' brought the tears
again and I prayed that God would give me a real
heart for those untouched by His love. I cry and
cry for lost friends and sometimes experience
tears with deep groaning that seems to come
from deep within my heart.

I expect people must think that I have deep
problems or huge burdens but these tears are not
for me (not anymore), but for lost and hurting
people. I thank God for these tears, embarrassing as it often is to 'sniff and dab', and yet
without these tears my heart would still be hard
and I never want that to happen again.

Cate's young life had been full of terrifying ordeals,
abuse and rejection. She had come to the conclusion
that there was no such thing as a loving God and tried
hard to bury any thoughts of Him. Some friends
invited Cate to a weekend of Christian events where
she spent much of the time talking with two young
students about her different experiences until she
suddenly felt something snap deep inside. She began
to weep. As her friends prayed, asking God to heal all
the hurt, fresh tears kept coming.

All the things that I had buried at the back of my
mind came flooding back and it was as if God
made me stand and face them. I was crying,

shaking and begging for Him to leave me alone but He didn't. God made me stand and face all the things, and all the people, that had ever hurt me, and in doing so He healed all the wounds that I had received. It was as if the tears washed it all away.

Since that night I haven't looked back! I know what it is like to be healed, albeit not in a physically obvious way. God has healed and blessed me through tears.

A number of people testify to the immediate release these healing tears bring. Some people have received hours of counselling that may not have brought obvious relief whereas in a prayerful situation the Holy Spirit has illuminated the deep traumas and memories bringing healing and release of these scars in an instant. Sometimes to carry out His work the Holy Spirit needs us to be prone, almost as though He is carrying out deep surgery on our hearts, and this is how Helen Watling found herself during a meeting.

I fell to the ground and began to cry and cry, although the entire time I was conscious of the Lord assuring me of His love. I had a picture in my mind of myself as a butterfly lying backwards in a pool of dirty water, unable to fly and bogged down by the filth. Later that night I had barely closed my eyes when I sensed God say, 'I am washing away the mud from your wings!'

The following day I again 'fell in the Spirit' but this time began to laugh and shake. My hands would not stop jumping up and down. I remember thinking how silly I must look to those around me, but it felt as though I was wired up to an electric current. I immediately had a picture of that television commercial rabbit advertising batteries – the rabbit that keeps clapping its cymbals together! I started laughing again and sensed the Lord saying, 'I am re-empowering you.' Then the picture of the butterfly returned again, but this time it was a vivid red and black variety. I knew this was called a 'Postman' butterfly and began to wonder, why?

A week later, as friends were praying together, I again began to cry, but this time I simply couldn't stop. As I lay there sobbing the Lord took me right back to a particular childhood nightmare, terrifying war-time memories, and other particularly painful happenings in later life. During this prayer time a friend was given a picture for my husband and myself, of two poppy heads full of seeds on thin, tall stems. I was immediately reminded of the poppy fields of Northern France and saw myself fighting across the mud and stench. There were dead and wounded everywhere and I sobbed in terror. Then the Lord said that He had known I would stand firm in the battles I'd been through but I had been hurt and wounded. As the tears eventually eased I sensed the words, 'Walk tall.' The following morning a verse from Psalm 126 floated into my head. 'Those who go forth crying, carrying good seed, will return, bringing their sheaves with them.' Something also made me look at an old copy of Bible reading notes by Selwyn Hughes and to my astonishment saw they were headed 'New Men – overnight'. In these notes were described the disciples' fear, insecurity and inferiority which had been completely routed when the Holy Spirit fell upon them (Acts 2). Hughes had written, 'A new power moved into them, cleansed the depths, reinforced all their natural faculties, co-ordinated them and made them unified persons.'

There were no more tears, but at the following Tuesday prayer meeting a further empowering by the Holy Spirit brought again the picture of my 'Postman' butterfly. Now I was free to fly. I could be the 'postman' that God wanted me to be, to take His love everywhere.

I met up with Helen at a conference about a year after she had written this. We spoke for only a moment but it was evident that the 'Postman butterfly' was still clearly 'in flight' as she had such a lovely air of freedom about her. And that's what it's really all about! Freedom to express the emotion and true feelings that God made us with and thereby repairing any damage as it occurs.

We have a greenhouse attached to the side of our house that became very damaged after a number of storms and high winds. The guttering had fallen off and some of the panes of glass had cracked and shattered, causing many leaks that dripped on to the brickwork inside making the walls all slimy green and mildewy. Where blooming geraniums should have been there was only a spreading pond-like variety of weed.

I had been recommended a 'Mr Smith' to come and put all this to rights. After a couple of days' work, masses of cups of tea and setting the world straight, Mr Smith said, 'Right, I'll be off then, Mrs Sheldon!' The way he had packed up all his tools made me realise that this was not just another tea-break but he meant he was off for good! 'But what about the *inside* of the greenhouse, Mr Smith?' I asked with alarm.

Our initial negotiations had included painting and repairing inside as well so reluctantly he agreed to come back the next day. Mr Smith turned up as if nothing had happened, and after his first cup of tea for the day he rather sheepishly handed me a gift as a silent apology. 'These are six of me best tomata plants,' he said proudly. The finished greenhouse looked lovely and the tomato plants grew and grew, giving us the most delicious crop of small, sweet cherry tomatoes.

Jesus paid the price for a completed job too. He didn't just pay for the outside of our lives to look good and sparkling and He is the only one who can really finish off the job inside. And Jesus gives us more. Like the tomato plants He gives us gifts. Those little cherry tomatoes didn't all ripen at the same time. Some were sweeter than others, some bigger than others, some the children ate, some we gave away, and some we kept to enjoy for ourselves. So it is with our healing and completion inside. It's ongoing. Sometimes our tears are just for us, often they are for others to share, but the harvest goes on and on.

I know from being in a wheelchair and physically dependent on others that real healing and freedom came, not when I got out of the wheelchair but when I asked God to forgive me and to help me forgive others. It was, of course, wonderful to be physically healed on the outside but I soon sensed God saying, 'Well, you've got your perfect working ballerina body back again, but what really needs healing is your heart and spirit inside.'

I once met a lady called Margaret who had been in a wheelchair since she was a child. She told me how she longed to take her able-bodied friends along to healing services. 'The trouble is, Julie, everyone always clamours around *me* to lay hands on *me*, and then they start to pray for *me* to be healed and raised out of the wheelchair!' The assumption was that Margaret couldn't possibly be *happy* being disabled. Actually, she was one of the most lovely, peaceful and holy women that I have ever met. Her focus and heart were truly on the Lord and she *was* happy in her chair.

'These wheels are my shoes,' she said.

I would have loved to have known such peace when I was disabled, but I'm thankful now that the healing took place the other way round as I realise the folly of putting all importance on physical healing: 'When I'm better it'll be all right. Everything will be fine when I can walk again.' In fact it wasn't and the feeling of being emotionally disabled was *far* worse than not being able to walk or feed myself. I really believe the true healing happened from the inside out.

7

The Gift of Tears

Who has the wisdom to count the drops of rain
or the tears that flow from heartfelt pain?
As rain comes from the heavens to water the
*   earth,*
do tears come from the eyes to water the heart?

It is God who tips over the water jars from the
*   heavens.*
It is He who put the tears into the soul.
It is He who designed tears to flow from the
*   eyes.*
It is He who waters the Spirit to grow in our
*   lives.*

So what are tears but a language all of their
*   own*
between God the Creator to mankind on earth?
They are the unspoken and unspeakable words

of wisdom,
our hearts speaking to His heart,
and once shared with Him, He is with us!

Joan Morris

My husband, Tom, and I had arrived early at the pretty New England church and were immediately struck by the whiteness of the building. The bright, white wooden clapperboard outside and the white pews inside gave it a fresh, clean appearance, but also there was the warmth and welcome one feels in a family home.

The pastor and his wife had earlier entertained us in their home. As they beavered about preparing for the evening service, Tom and I sat in a pew to enjoy our surroundings. I had been invited to speak about my healing at the meeting, and I was grateful to have a moment in which to get the feel of the church, and also to have time for the calming of the butterflies that wake from their slumbers on such occasions. The need to 'Be still, and know that I am God' has become more and more vital to me before each talk I give, and the 'still small voice of calm' needs a chance to be heard as well. I had spoken at nine churches in ten days in Connecticut, so this much-needed stillness was precious.

My attention, however, was suddenly caught by Carol, the pastor's wife, walking up the aisle carrying a box of paper hankies. This was no ordinary box of tissues. These were American king-size giant tissues!

I was fascinated to watch Carol take great wads from the box and place them at the ends of each padded pew. Tom also had noticed this, and looked at me with a rather puzzled expression. By the time she reached our pew we just had to ask, 'Carol, what *are* you doing?'

With great aplomb she plonked our allotted pile of tissues down and replied, 'We're expecting Jesus tonight. And when the Holy Spirit of God arrives, so do the *tears*!'

During the recent charismatic renewal, tears have been a feature. This has led to a certain amount of confusion, as some Christians have talked of the 'gift of tears' as though tears were given by the Holy Spirit to build up the church, as are spiritual gifts of teaching or prophecy, for example. It is not possible, working solely from biblical texts, to argue that tears are a spiritual gift, because the New Testament lists of gifts of the Holy Spirit do not include tears.

However, many people have experienced tears as an unmerited – and often unsought – gift, which they acknowledge as coming from God. For them tears are a source of personal blessing which has released or healed them, freeing them to serve God as more whole people than they were before. It is in the sense that some tears are a present, as it were, from God, generously given for the good of all God's people, that I understand tears to be a gift, and here refer to the gift of tears.

Tears can be induced by slicing onions, or may

accompany or express blind rage, wallowing self-pity, deep sympathy, sorrow or laughter. We have, therefore, to avoid labelling every experience of crying as a gift of tears. Even when tears are received as a gift from God, it is important to remember that they are neither a reward for long service, nor a sign of maturity (or immaturity). The gift speaks only of the Giver's generosity, not the receiver's merit.

Christians in Eastern Orthodox churches use many names to describe the gift of tears. Among these are: the way of tears; the prayer of tears; the gift of tears; holy sadness; tears which illuminate; and weeping without ceasing. In *The Orthodox Way* (St Vladimir's Seminary Press), Bishop Kallistos Ware writes:

> When it is genuinely spiritual, 'speaking with tongues' seems to represent an act of 'letting go' – the crucial moment in the breaking down of our self-trust, and its willingness to allow God to act within us. In the Orthodox tradition this act of 'letting go' . . . often takes the form of the gift of tears.

So although tears feature in the writings of Augustine, Mother Julian, St Francis and other Christians from the West, it may be that it is from the Christians of the East (who have never had to 'rediscover' the Holy Spirit, because they never 'lost' Him) that the richest experience and teaching about the gift of tears comes.

John Richards has experienced tears in a wide

variety of contexts, but says that the experience of the gift of tears comes within a different category. He found that the gift was rarely linked to any emotional change, but the tears just came, with no feeling of weeping or crying. The occasions of their coming were quite exclusively the times when God was particularly present by His Spirit. The tears came in times both of receiving and giving ministry; in times of prayer, and during times of worship. He felt there was only any sense of weeping accompanying these tears when he felt an overshadowing of either wonder or pain. On one occasion, he recalls, at the 1975 Westminster Conference, he found himself, with many others, weeping in a way quite unrelated to normal crying – his shirt was completely drenched.

John also recounts the time when a minister came to him, appearing deeply troubled, because although he had experienced a baptism in the Holy Spirit he had not received the gift of tongues. 'Perhaps you have the gift of tears,' John suggested. A burden seemed visibly to lift from the minister as he replied, 'I've never heard of such a thing, but if it exists then I have certainly received it!'

Until relatively recently, few Christians in the West have looked at tears as being a gift, something to treasure for oneself or to give away to others. Joan Morris feels the whole concept of tears has changed.

I really don't think they are a new thing. It just is that nowadays people seem more prepared to let them flow, whereas years ago it wasn't quite the 'done thing'! Even today there are some people who negatively criticise them! I have cried for all sorts of reasons since I was a small child – sad, happy, anxious – you name it, I've cried. I have tried to hide my tears, suppress them and even curse them. Now, as a Christian, I covet them like a precious gift from God Himself. Now I find I can pray through them and I trust God to use these tears. I am drawn to people who cry and then I find myself crying with them! I believe God uses this as a sign that I can share that person's pain and that I really care. Tears are a gift that I can pass on.

Joyce used to think that people saw her as a person full of trouble and she felt embarrassed:

Sometimes I had only to walk into church and the Holy Spirit would touch me and I would start weeping. The words of a hymn or worship song would catch me out! At one time I even asked God to 'please take the tears away'. He did. I began to become a hard person again and I ended up being so sorry and asking for this gift of tears to be given back. I had asked God to teach me to pray and this He did, but not my way. He did it through tears. The thing is it catches me out at the most unexpected times now. I can even be at the kitchen sink and unexpectedly the tears will start to come up from deep down and I have to retreat to my room. Sometimes I don't even know what the tears are for, but I am learning to let God have His way because He knows and I don't need an explanation!

These tears are not just of compassion or repentance. They can be tears of indescribable joy, just being one with God. I now treasure this gift and would encourage others to do the same because if people see you weeping you don't know how that will touch their hearts and draw them to God. If in doubt find a quiet place for a few minutes and let the tears of love flow and thank God for His gift and tell Him you are willing to serve Him through tears.

Perhaps if we can begin to view tears as a gift from God instead of an inconvenience we will feel more free to express this emotion. Norma Taziker, who has had great tragedy in her life, said, 'I never thought of tears being a gift from the Lord because whenever I enter into His presence I always have tears in my eyes and I try to hold them back. But from now on I will let them go!'

'I have never heard of the "gift of tears" before and naturally I am more than curious!' Dee Harrison recalled that for as long as she can remember hardly a Sunday has gone by without her having leaky eyes during a service. From greeting someone at the door, during the praise and worship, taking communion, listening to the sermon and prayers, to chatting with people afterwards, the tears can flow. She told me,

> I have despaired of this 'leaky eye syndrome', and now only use waterproof mascara because I got so fed up with the black streaks criss-crossing my face so regularly. The tears can be just a few little drops or even great gushes. Sometimes, but not always, I know certain songs can trigger them off. I literally melt at the awesomeness and greatness of Jesus and our Father God, and this reduces me to tears of overwhelming thankfulness.
>
> At other times tears just fill up my eyes and spill out. I try to avoid 'being noticed' and rather than dab at them I just let them run their course which leads to various consequences of wet ears, wet collars and wet shoes! Often I am convinced I'm the only person in the congregation who is experiencing this 'fallout', and I've stopped apologising. As for all this being a gift? I've tried being analytical; praying to have my tears dry up; pleading that upon entering a meeting I could have a 'tear-free time'. So far none of these have been successful and I have resolved to being tearful more often than not.

Most gifts and presents are gratefully received and the 'gift of tears' is one to be welcomed, used and passed on to others. Lyndall Hacker describes herself as 'one of the damp hanky brigade' but has been deeply reassured of the truth that God 'controls' our weeping.

A couple of days before my father died I had the privilege of leading him to Jesus Christ. I was dry-eyed throughout the precious time we had together talking and praying, whereas usually I would have been extremely damp! During the final moments of his life there were about eight of us with my father. The others, including the men, wept openly for the passing of a lovely man, but I found myself being the mouthpiece for expressing their final messages of love and speaking out words from Scripture. It really showed me that I can trust God for my tears, and that they can be used as a gift when needed.

Hilary Swallow gives a beautiful account of tears being used and given as a gift, although the person concerned felt he had been of absolutely no use to the people in need:

A family from America arrived in our church and very quickly they became much loved and cared for in the community. Their youngest daughter developed measles and instead of the disease taking its normal course, complications arose and the little girl was extremely ill. It was such a shock to the whole church when news came of the little girl's death. Children are not expected to die from measles in this country.

The rector of the church immediately visited the bereaved parents and on arriving at their home found that he had no words to say. He was overcome by sorrow, so much so that his tears flowed. He eventually returned home, chastising himself for being so ineffective to this dear family in their grief.

Later, after the funeral, the parents of the little girl thanked the rector for all his kindness and sympathy. They explained to him how his *tears* had comforted them more than any words could possibly have done. He had shown real empathy with their pain.

This type of weeping comes with deep compassion and if these tears are a gift from God, then I believe He gives with them a fleeting glimpse of what He feels for His people.

Gill, a vicar's wife, wrote that the whole question of the gift of tears has caused her to ponder, especially since the summer and autumn of 1994.

The times of specific intercession for people have been marked by tears, great floods of tears that flow for ages. As I'm married to the vicar, have people floating in and out of the home and have five children, I'm careful about when and where I pray these days! On one occasion I cried, utterly broken-heartedly, for the whole of the ministry session within the church service. This was to the consternation of all around. I was clucked and fussed over, reassured, told it was 'all too much' and generally was on the receiving end of a *lot* of sympathy. It sounds cruel, but it was all in vain. I was not crying because I was sad . . . or mad . . . or bad, but simply for the reason that, for a second, God gave me an insight into how *He* felt for a person sitting nearby.

I'm not a person who likes attention. I prefer to hide behind my husband, children, the font, the Sunday school – in fact, anything! But this weeping, this howling, was hard to hide. This type of thing has happened again and again. Because it's new to me I've been very discreetly checking out what was going on in other people's lives at the times I 'go moist'. In all the cases, so far, the people I am weeping for have reached a decision point in their lives. Something is causing a barrier between them and God, and they don't want, or can't, move it. They are wrestling with God and feeling as if He doesn't like, or love, them very much. At the time of this weeping I feel as if I am begging and pleading for God to break through, even when these other people are nowhere near me. This makes little sense to me. Indeed, I am not certain I can theologically back it up – or can I?

At other times I find myself weeping over the state of some areas of the world. Interestingly, it's not usually the big traumatic ones, but at these times it feels as though God empties a bucket over my head – and I cry, out of nowhere. It feels (again, this is all so very experiential) as though something is being 'poured out', 'laid down', 'given', and that something is moving in the heavens.

I rest secure in the knowledge that were we ever to meet I am the last person you would associate with having the 'gift or ministry of tears'. I'm not that kind of person! However, Isaiah 55:8–9 springs to mind rather quickly! 'For my thoughts are not your thoughts, neither are your ways my ways,' declares the Lord. 'As the heavens are higher than the earth, so are my ways higher than your ways and my thoughts than your thoughts.'

Bernard would place the gift of tears in the context of his overall spiritual journey, which includes the feminine aspects of his personality developing to balance up the masculine traits. He said, 'This is an even greater marvel than tears and is much more relevant to my ability to reach out to other people.' As a married man having had a career mainly as a manager or business consultant in 'high tech' industries, he was aware that his basic skills include an analytical, logical brain. Yet, for the past ten years, tears have been a normal part of his prayer life.

My prayer style is not extrovert or charismatic. It is quite the opposite, mainly being deeply contemplative and often wordless. There are occasions when this gift of tears just happens while I am praying, either by myself in my daily prayer time, or with others – much to their surprise! When someone prays over me I sometimes just burst and weep, for between a few minutes and half an hour. It doesn't always happen like this but the reason I weep is quite clear to me. I am being blessed by the Holy Spirit. Usually I know why I am being blessed and this comes with the tears. Sometimes it is reassurance that I am on the right path, but more often it is a strengthening for some task I have been called upon to do. Other times I don't know what the tears are for but then I tend to assume that I am being blessed for something that lies ahead.

I cannot predict when I will weep, and I cannot bring on tears. I don't feel very emotional beforehand, and don't weep when praying for those in distress or any other situations. These tears are more likely to happen when I meet people in a bad life situation and I find myself being filled with compassion for that person.

Dr Tony Stead said:

> I think many of us, especially we men, keep this
> gift and blessing to ourselves and often dismiss
> it as emotionalism. I believe we all need to
> empty ourselves and open our hearts to what our
> Lord is saying to us so we can hear His voice
> with the 'ears of our heart'.

'Like many men of my generation and culture I had
been taught that crying was a sign of self-indulgent
weakness.' So began the account from Kevin Allison.

> My Royal Air Force (RAF) years had, of course,
> reinforced that thought and I had learned to hide
> my emotions on the many occasions when I had
> found myself on the brink of tears. I didn't
> analyse it at the time but things that made me
> want to cry were not fear or pain, but incidents
> which confronted me with extremes of beauty in
> creation, goodness, kindness, gentleness, joy,
> peace, patience, faithfulness, self-control and
> love . . . and I knew nothing about Galatians
> 5:22–3!
>
> I became very adept at hiding my feelings
> especially during the years my wife, Olive,
> suffered much illness, but was brought up
> sharply one morning when I was told about a
> number of young people who were praying for
> us. 'That's nice,' I thought as I continued to eat

breakfast. Then suddenly it was as though someone had wrapped a lovely warm blanket of love around me, and I burst into tears and sobbed and sobbed. I was completely amazed by the experience but viewed it in purely psychological terms as I had been under great emotional strain. I assumed that this was simply one of those 'triggers' which release pent-up emotions, yet I was also conscious that there was something about it which was of a different quality to anything I had experienced before.

I was due to go and photograph a soccer match, and found myself weeping all the way there in the car. At the game I sat on the touch-line (well away from my colleagues) and wept so much I couldn't focus the camera. All the way home I wept and struggled to understand what on earth was going on, because far from feeling sad I found myself full of joy and peace! However, I didn't tell my wife anything about the experience – it wasn't British and I didn't want to upset her.

Two years later, a bishop came to our church and gave a talk about the Christian healing ministry. Within *minutes* I was sobbing my heart out again. To my surprise, the bishop seemed to be, however gently and lovingly, absolutely chuffed (that is RAF-speak for delighted) with my tears! Since that time he has taught me a great deal about weeping, but it hasn't always, and still isn't, easy to allow God to release this gift in and through me.

As time has gone by I have found this gift has brought some very significant personal changes. For example, when I find myself confronted by an angry person I no longer respond with my anger. I am overcome with God's love for that person and my first thought is, 'Please, Lord, show me why they are like this.' In an argument I am less inclined to want to win it at all costs – I have a quick wit and a biting tongue – and am more inclined to try and cool things down and open up the discussion. I am learning to back off when I see that someone else needs to defeat me. Very often now I find myself moved to tears. This rarely produces negative responses and somehow people know these are not mani-pulative tears, or tears of weakness.

I have been contacted by people who have said that my tears have led them, at some point, to recognise a particular problem that needs to be dealt with, and this seems to be particularly the case with other men. A number of times I have been told that the tears had finally cracked their hearts and enabled God to draw them to Himself.

Sometimes when praying on a one-to-one basis with people in need I find myself praying with tears for them when they are unable to cry themselves. Often my tears release them into weeping. Sometimes the sense of God's love for them is almost unbearable and they need to feel and know it. At other times the tears are of laughter and joy. Often I can't find any explanations for my tears, and then I simply have to offer them to Jesus and trust that He knows what He is doing. I have a sneaky feeling that then He is ministering to me and it isn't good for me to understand, at that point, what He is doing.

Praying intercessions in church often brings me to tears. In our church, intercessors are required to write out their prayers and read them. I can write out these prayers without turning a hair and sometimes I can read them in the approved Anglican manner. But when I'm least expecting it that warm blanket descends and I'm off again with tears. And, would you believe it, even men in an Anglican congregation can weep!

One recognises that, like any other gift, it is open to misuse and I try to keep myself open to the purely psychological aspects and not become sentimental, attention-seeking, manipulative and so on. I pray daily that with integrity I may be able to say, 'I am a fool for Jesus's and I ask of those I meet, 'Please be patient, God hasn't finished with me yet!'

There was a time when I was getting very ill, very fast, and my parents, David and Jean Mumford, invited a couple to supper. After the meal they enquired about my health and wanted to know all the details. The wife of the couple listened intently and suddenly started to weep – gently at first and then more and more intensely. She fell to her knees and wept with her head between her hands on the floor. My mother recalls how this seemed very holy and special, and none of them did anything to stop her or comfort her.

After at least a quarter of an hour, maybe more, the wife gently stopped sobbing and sat on her chair. She explained that my suffering went deeply to her heart, and the tears came and just would not stop. She seemed exhausted afterwards so my parents brought the evening to a close with prayer and bade them goodbye.

As my mother returned to the sitting room to tidy up she suddenly saw a dark patch on the pale green carpet. She kneeled down to touch it. The carpet was soaking wet. She realised it was a pool of tears, a soggy circle of about six inches in diameter. My mother remembers: 'It touched me greatly that someone could weep so profusely for someone else's daughter, my daughter. I could never forget that incident.'

When, with the Holy Spirit, we see situations and people through the eyes of Jesus, and with the empathy of His compassionate heart, then we will leave pools of tears behind us.

Up until three years ago Heidi Frankland would not

have considered or called tears a gift; there had been many occasions when it had felt much more like a curse. As a young girl of twelve, Heidi made a specific and determined effort not to cry in front of her mother and younger sister. They were all watching an old sentimental film on television at the end of which Heidi's mother and sister were crying, yet she remembers holding in her tears and vowing to herself not to weep publicly. Over the years she found the tears had a way of wanting to come out in spite of her best efforts to suppress them, particularly as she began to learn in high school about the Holocaust, Vietnam and all other atrocities of war. As time went by seeing acts of kindness, heroism or bravery, especially watching the competitors in the Special Olympics displaying their determination and courage, would have the same effect.

Looking back I'm sure a lot of this was due to growing up and maturing. But I also feel God was shaking me up and putting me back in touch with my cold emotions. After training as a nurse, specialising in looking after people with cancer, I found I would sometimes cry with patients and their families. A part of me would say, 'Well, that's not very professional', but I could see how much it helped, how the tears comforted more than words, so I tried to ignore the nagging doubts.

Emotions gradually became a less forbidden

zone but I still found tears confusing. One Easter Sunday morning, the first one after the death of my dearly loved grandmother, and the trauma of a recent divorce, I decided to go to church. I had been a churchgoer most of my life and this particular morning chose a church I hadn't been to before. To my great consternation I found myself crying the minute I walked through the door. What would all these people think? I couldn't sing any of the hymns and slipped quickly away at the end of the service so I wouldn't have to speak to anyone. As I reflected on the morning's events I was left wondering what was going on because for a number of years a gifted preacher, certain Bible passages, services at Christmas, Good Friday and Easter had all been having a similar effect. I just could not understand how thinking, hearing or singing about God or Jesus could make a person cry, and I was totally unaware of anyone else having a similar experience.

There was an increasing desire to spend more time with God but I had no idea this would come about through illness. I swung between feeling like I had crashed head-on into a wall, to a completely flat battery! Bit by bit over the following year God changed my life by restoring me in body, mind and spirit. I was certainly due for a major overhaul in all areas!

With the repair work in progress I recall

starting to feel like a giant sponge, soaking up all I could read and hear about God and this led me to a conference where the speaker began to talk about the Holy Spirit. The moment the talk started so did my tears! 'Oh no,' I thought. 'Not here, everyone will see. I feel so embarrassed!' I tried holding back but it was as if a dam was waiting to burst. I gave in. The fight was over. What a relief! That day transformed my life as the tears flowed out and the Holy Spirit flowed in.

From that moment on I would still often feel foolish and embarrassed crying in front of other people, but it was almost too painful not to cry. A chance remark from a friend about the 'gift of tears' changed something in me and I began to see these tears in a different light and I wanted to know more of how God might use them. This funny 'gift' that was feeling like a burden or curse began to unearth new understanding and on hearing the words: 'We all come from different backgrounds but we are all *one body*', I felt God speaking directly to my spirit: 'When you hear an absolute *truth* you will have *tears*.' This reassuring promise has been true ever since and I am beginning to learn about God's heart through this gift of tears. Sometimes the weeping is for me. At other times it is for individuals, groups and situations. Psalm 126:5–6 has been fulfilled: 'Those who sow in

tears will reap with songs of joy. He who goes
out weeping, carrying seed to sow, will return
with songs of joy, carrying sheaves with him.'

Heidi offers a very helpful list of the ways she sees
this 'gift of tears' being of use.

Tears soften, cleanse and purify my heart.
Tears soften hard ground, removing barriers and
thereby helping other people to weep.
Tears unburden and set people free.
Tears release the Holy Spirit and allow Him to
enter the situation.
Tears are feeling God's love, either for me, for a
specific person or for a group of people.
Tears are experiencing God's compassion; His
pain and sorrow.
Tears are of overwhelming joy, thanksgiving and
rejoicing in the Lord and thinking of who He is
and how He suffered for me.
Tears are to thank Jesus for all He is doing, and
will do, in my life and the lives of other people.
Tears are for finding lost sheep, for the joy of
someone giving their life to Christ. The other
side of this is weeping over those who are still
lost, and the compassion, sorrow and pain that
is God's.
Tears are hearing an absolute truth.

Heidi concludes that she would not have chosen this

gift! But she is learning to trust God's methods and is thankful that she cannot manufacture, or turn on at will, these tears. By accepting, opening, and using this particular gift she surely will 'gather the harvest with joy'!

When I have told my story of being healed from dystonia, many people have responded with tears. But as I have chatted to such people on a one-to-one basis after my talk, once the drips have been mopped up and the soggy tissues hidden, the apologies have begun. 'I'm so sorry. Isn't this silly? I haven't cried for years. I don't know what came over me. It's so selfish of me to cry. There are so many other people worse off than I am. I mustn't complain. There's so much to be thankful for . . .'

At first I used to sympathise with people who said things like this to me, understanding completely their embarrassment at crying in a public meeting. But I have come to believe that people need more than sympathy when they have cried. They need encouragement to regard tears as a normal part of life. When we cry, somehow we begin to regain emotional balance. Tears are a sign of restoration, cleansing and wholeness. The tendency from childhood memories to associate them with weakness is a great hindrance to the emotional health God wants to give everyone.

Speaking in public about my healing makes me feel very vulnerable. I am not a trained speaker, and I always feel very inadequate beforehand. But my longing to tell other people how much God has done for me, and more than that, the possibility that they might come to know Jesus Christ for themselves, propels me to ask Him on each occasion for the words to reach the next crowd of strangers to whom I speak. I have realised that some people who hear me and cry are in fact responding to my willingness to be seen as vulnerable. It is as if me telling my story acts as a trigger, releasing their guard, and allowing them to show their real feelings, even if that involves the social embarrassment of crying.

To this day, I continue to find myself weeping in prayer, over all sorts of people and situations. I am convinced tears are a blessing. God bless you through your tears.

Afterword

We've just celebrated our younger daughter's eighteenth birthday.

You may recall at the beginning of this book I mentioned how our daughter had become seriously ill during the writing of *The Blessing of Tears*. She was two weeks into being ten years old when the diagnosis was made of a malignant brain tumour.

And here we are, eight years later, having celebrated with cake and tears. During these eight years there have been tears of thankfulness, relief, amazement at her courage and will to survive, and tears of mourning for her friend Ross who recently died, aged fourteen, of a similar tumour after battling for those eight years.

But there also have been tears that have no names: tears that express such depth of feelings that none of us can really describe them. God helped us through yesterday. We're trusting God for today. And we may cry again tomorrow.

Julie Sheldon
September 2003

Further Reading

Richard Foster, *Prayer: Finding the Heart's True Home*, especially Chapter 4, 'The Prayer of Tears', Hodder and Stoughton, 1992.

Arthur Wallis, *Pray in the Spirit*, especially Chapter 16, 'Travail and Tears', Kingsway, 1970.

Acknowledgments

'Citizens of heaven' by Marilyn Baker, 1995, quoted by kind permission (*as seen on page 41*).

'Summoned by Bells' by John Betjeman. Used by kind permission of John Murray (Publishers) Ltd (*as seen on page 50*).

Poem from *Mending* by Dorothy Hsu, 1988, copyright © Christian Literature Crusade, Fort Washington, Pennsylvania, USA. Used by kind permission (*as seen on page 13*).

'There is a Redeemer' by Melody Green, 1982, copyright © Birdwing Music/BMG Songs Inc./ Alliance Media Ltd. Administered by CopyCare, PO Box 77, Hailsham BN27 3EF. Used by kind permission (*as seen on page 39*).